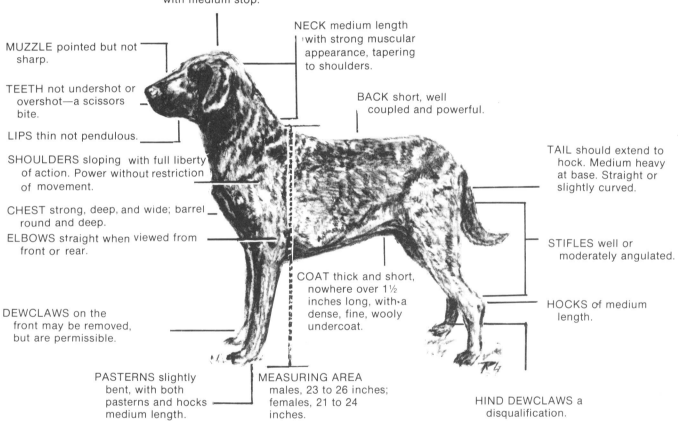

SKULL broad and round with medium stop.

NECK medium length with strong muscular appearance, tapering to shoulders.

MUZZLE pointed but not sharp.

TEETH not undershot or overshot—a scissors bite.

LIPS thin not pendulous.

SHOULDERS sloping with full liberty of action. Power without restriction of movement.

CHEST strong, deep, and wide; barrel round and deep.

ELBOWS straight when viewed from front or rear.

BACK short, well coupled and powerful.

TAIL should extend to hock. Medium heavy at base. Straight or slightly curved.

STIFLES well or moderately angulated.

COAT thick and short, nowhere over 1½ inches long, with a dense, fine, wooly undercoat.

HOCKS of medium length.

DEWCLAWS on the front may be removed, but are permissible.

PASTERNS slightly bent, with both pasterns and hocks medium length.

MEASURING AREA males, 23 to 26 inches; females, 21 to 24 inches.

HIND DEWCLAWS a disqualification.

The Chesapeake Bay Retriever

By Arthur S. Beaman

Edited By
William W. Denlinger and R. Annabel Rathman

Cover design by
Bob Groves

DENLINGER'S PUBLISHERS, LTD.
Box 76, Fairfax, Virginia 22030

The scent of a skunk excites the curiosity of this young Chessie!

Library of Congress Cataloging in Publication Data
Beaman, Arthur S.
    The Chesapeake Bay retriever.

    1. Chesapeake Bay Retrievers. I. Denlinger,
        William Watson.
II. Rathman, R. Annabel. III. Title.
SF429.C4B4   636.7'52   80-69084
ISBN O-87714-075-8   AACR2

International Standard Book Number: 0-87714-075-8
Library of Congress Catalog Card Number: 80-69084

The author, Arthur S. Beaman, with Spinner.

Spinner relaxes in the dentist's chair.

Foreword

For a long time, I have had it in my mind to write a book on one of the Retriever breeds. Upon researching books on the three most popular Retrievers, I found, to my surprise, that no comprehensive book had ever been written about the Chesapeake. Therefore, I almost automatically made my choice.

I find it difficult to write about the Chesapeake—especially since I have raised and trained both Labradors and Goldens, and in my mind I must compare them to Chesapeakes. This would not be true if I had raised only Chesapeakes.

However, although you might disagree violently with what I say, I'm sure you will find much food for thought.

The Chesapeake is intensely loyal and basically a one-man dog. This very loyalty and resultant possessiveness have tended to inhibit this fine breed's adjustment to the increasingly crowded conditions of modern-day life.

Although the Chesapeake springs from the same origins as does the Labrador, the latter was developed in Great Britain by the landed gentry. He had to get along in large kennels, had to be well-mannered and easily controlled, and had to conform generally to the rather ritualized grouse and pheasant drives developed to a high degree in that land.

Conversely, the Chesapeake was designed to prosper in a very different world. This was the domain of the lonely professional market hunter of the nineteenth century and early years of the twentieth century along the Atlantic seaboard. The Chesapeake's abode was no well-ordered kennel. His nest was probably a pile of sacking outside his owner's shack on the marsh. He was not typically associated with other dogs, or with humans other than his owner. His first and foremost job was to retrieve, in whatever fashion appealed to him, many tens and even hundreds of waterfowl crippled or killed at one time by the enormous "punt gun." His second job, perhaps no less important, was to guard his owner's hut and equipment during the absences required for marketing the game. There were no sheriffs or game wardens in those areas then, and the hunters themselves were not above easing their lot by appropriating necessities from others. It is not hard to understand, then, that to the desire and ability to retrieve, preserved from his early ancestors, this dog also acquired the thick, oily coat so necessary to protect him in his work and his rest, and whether or not the aroma was pleasant had no import. Then, too, the one-man nature of the Chesapeake, the protective attitude, and the desire to stay home and not wander, were obvious necessities.

The efforts of today's fanciers to breed Chesapeakes which can fit into the average household with a family of kids, with next-door neighbors, and with numbers of strangers coming into the house as guests, delivery men, meter readers, postmen, and others, have been entirely successful in some instances, partially so in others, and not so successful in still others.

Through the years, my wife and I have had many good Chesapeakes, always intelligent and usually easygoing. A few did not fit into the latter category, but you will read about them in this book.

One tends to remember the good and forget the others, but I'm not that kind of writer.

The Chesapeake Bay Retriever is a marvelous breed of dog. Like humans, Chesapeakes have many extremely strong points, and like humans, they have their share of weak ones—and these they come by naturally.

It is my hope that this book not only will make many new friends for the Chesapeake, but also will be helpful to Chesapeake fanciers everywhere in their efforts to enhance the truly remarkable qualities of this fine animal, and to select away from those qualities not fully compatible with society as it exists today. It is precisely in these areas that the popularity of Chesapeakes as a breed will continue to be increased. Read on!!!

A.S.B.

Acknowledgements

So many people helped me with this book that it would be impossible to list all of them. However, I would like especially to acknowledge the assistance of the late Helen Fleischmann from California, who supplied information about her Mount Joy Kennels plus many excellent photographs; Rainey Weremiechik, an old friend and Regional Director of the American Chesapeake Club, who provided much information and moral support; and last but far from least, my good wife Ruth and my good friend Bob Massaroni, who patiently both posed and snapped many of the photos. Thank you all, and many others. BUT, I dedicate this book to one who grew up with the writing and today is the most magnificent companion and hunting dog, our Chesapeake,

SPINNER THE GRINNER!!!

Contents

South Bay Nike, handled by author Arthur S. Beaman, places first. May 9, 1965.

A. M. COGHLIN'S CLAIRVINE

THE LATE DR. MILBANK'S PRIDE

THE LATE DR. MILBANK'S BUSH

THE LATE MR. MALLORY'S MARY

CHIEF
Owned by J. G. McPhee, Seattle

PEGGIE MAGUIRE
Owned by McFee & Gilbert, Seattle

CHESAPEAKE BAY DOGS OF MARYLAND, OHIO AND THE PACIFIC COAST

From *The Dog Book*, by James Watson, 1906.

The Chesapeake Bay Retriever

The Chesapeake Bay Retriever enjoys two distinctions above all other Retrievers, and one above all other Sporting breeds.

First, the Chesapeake is the only Sporting Dog developed in the United States. Be that by accident or design, the proof is there. Second, he is by far the best of the Retriever breeds in heavy seas, in icy waters, in actual ice floes, in marshes, and in all situations calling for waterfowl retrieving in difficult circumstances.

The beginning and evolution of the Chesapeake are not shrouded in as much mystery as are those of other Sporting breeds. We know the date of the beginning; we know the evolution as it is told in two fairly plausible versions; and we know pretty much what happened later. So let us begin.

It is a well-known fact that during the year 1807, the Chesapeake breed was born. The story that is told most often concerns the ship *Canton*, which was sailing from Baltimore on its way to Liverpool. The crew hailed a British brig that had run aground while plying its trade between Newfoundland and England. While the British seamen were being rescued, two dogs also were taken aboard the *Canton*.

The male dog was named "Sailor," and the bitch was named "Canton," after the rescuing vessel.

The dog was black and the bitch a dirty brown color. Dr. James Stuart of Sparrows Point, Maryland, was very kind and helpful to the British seamen. To show their gratitude, they presented the two dogs to him. Sparrows Point was quite near Baltimore and on the Chesapeake Bay, and Dr. Stuart was an ardent hunter of waterfowl. He lost no time in discovering that his two new dogs were superlative retrievers. In no time at all, bitches of all descriptions arrived to be bred to Sailor. Many of these were of the common yellow Coonhound variety, and it is thought that the varying shades of brown in the Chesapeake evolved from the Coonhound matings. Sailor, presumably, was bred to Canton, although there is no positive record of matings of the two. Pups from such matings are believed to have been kept by Dr. Stuart and probably were guarded jealously from other hunters. I would guess that the progeny would have been bred and rebred together, with the weak being discarded and the strong retained.

Remember, both Sailor and Canton presumably had all of the qualities sought in retrievers. They were said to be rough, tough dogs that would battle the ice-filled waters of the Chesapeake Bay for hours just to retrieve a single duck or goose. Having very strong, muscular necks and big mouths, they could handle the largest birds with ease.

Eventually, but at least by 1885, a distinct Chesapeake breed had been established.

Another theory of the evolution of the Chesapeake breed is bandied about a good deal among hunters of the Chesapeake Bay area. It was first related by an elderly gentleman, General Latrobe, a respected and long-time hunter of waterfowl in Maryland.

According to General Latrobe, a Newfoundland vessel was stranded on the Maryland shore, and the two dogs on board (lesser Newfoundlands) were presented to a Mr. George Law, who helped the captain and his crew a great deal during their trying time. The General insists that both of the dogs were crossed only with the common Coonhound of that day. The color might bear him out, but I am sure that they would also have been bred to other breeds, as well as to each other.

Either account might be correct, but the true story probably balances out between the two. Many people are of the opinion that the Chesapeake was originally the deadgrass or sedge color, but this is not true. The original Chesapeake was of a dark brown color. The deadgrass color did not come into the picture until many years later.

Whichever account is correct, one occurrence forever shrouds the actual origin in mystery. During the latter part of the nineteenth century, there existed a club known as the Carroll Island Gun Club. The members bred Chesapeakes exclusively, and sportsmen came from all over the country just to shoot over these dogs and to see them retrieve. Unfortunately, in the early years of the twentieth century, there was a disastrous fire at the club and all of the Carroll Island breeding records were lost.

The early Chesapeake certainly lacked finish. He was far from pretty, but unlike many of today's Retrievers, he always got the job done. After all, in the mid-nineteenth century, there were very few bench shows, and hunters just wanted a dog that could retrieve, retrieve, retrieve. The Chesapeake was that.

The light yellow eye was another point of argument cited in General Latrobe's account of the origin of the breed, but this was proven false. According to geneticists who have studied color in dogs, the yellow eye went along with any shade of brown in the Chesapeake's coat. It was hereditary and irreversible. Today, a few of the darker colored dogs have a dark eye, but they may be just the exceptions that prove the rule. And I cannot see what difference the color of the eye makes in the retrieving ability.

By 1885, a definite type of dog had evolved, and curiously enough the deadgrass color was almost unknown. Reddish sedge to dark brown were the only colors, and the coat was longer and thicker than it is today. The length and thickness of the coat may have been dominant traits from the longer, heavier Newfoundland coat.

About 1910, the deadgrass color was developed in the Midwest because of a popular but erroneous theory that ducks and geese found it harder to spot the Retrievers when they blended into the hunting terrain. Many years later it was proven that color made no difference—that ducks and geese would decoy in just as well to a black dog as they would to any other color. But there are still some die-hards who dispute this.

It is very true, however, that the Chesapeake coat suffered greatly from the introduction of the deadgrass shade. It became shorter, was not as thick, and did not shed water nearly so well as the original coat.

In later years, the coat was improved once again by careful breeding, and today it is again more water repellent than the coat of any other Retriever breed.

The two foregoing accounts of the origin of the breed are the best substantiated, but it is obvious to any knowledgeable breeder that there must have been other blood infused to produce the Chesapeake of today.

The most obvious of the probable crosses are the Flat-Coated Retriever, the Curly-Coated Retriever, and the Irish Water Spaniel. I have found no record of the Flat-Coated Retriever in the Chesapeake Bay area during the nineteenth century. I bred Irish Water Spaniels in 1949 in the Chesapeake Bay area, and many old families told me that this was the first time the Irish had been introduced. This leaves the Curly-Coated Retriever as a possible forebear of the Chesapeake.

The Curly-Coated Retriever is much like the Chesapeake in disposition and ability. Both are rather slow, but very sure. Both have the tendency to not bring in cripples, and they do not mouth the birds as other breeds do. For an educated guess, I would say that the old Chesapeake has quite a bit of Curly-Coated Retriever blood—and it hasn't harmed him.

When the deadgrass color was introduced in the Midwest shortly before World War I, the Chesapeake was becoming very popular in that area. Two different types evolved. The one in the Midwest was smaller, with the deadgrass color. The other in the East was much larger, with the dark brown color. It was not until the late 1930s that one type started to emerge.

About 1885, many famous lines of Chesapeakes were developed. Besides the Carroll Island Gun Club strain, the great dogs of Earl Henry, founder of the Western Chesapeake, started to emerge. Also, William Hurst, manager of the famed Chesacroft Kennels, had started to produce some great dogs.

By the early 1930s, the Chesapeake had become very popular—more so than any other retrieving breed. A dog by the name of Sodaks Gypsy Prince was bred in Minnesota by Father Joseph Shuster. He was shipped to the East in time for the first Retriever trial in 1932. Prince was the first Chesapeake to win both his field and bench titles. He proved a prepotent stud and introduced into the breed both speed and style. When he was mated with the progeny of Skipper Bob, another great early Chesapeake, his descendants dominated the early field trials. Prince's name was found in almost every pedigree of the Chesapeakes placing in field trials during the first fifteen years such events were held.

In contrast with the speed demanded in field trials of today, judges of trials in the thirties and even the late forties often would call four or five dogs on line at one time. One bird, usually a very difficult single, would be shot and frequently was crippled. The judge would call a number. One of the four or five dogs on line would be sent, and the others would sit quietly, waiting and watching, or, to use the field trial term, "honoring." If, after a fair length of time, the first dog did not pick up the bird, the handler would be asked to call in his dog, and another dog from the same line would be sent. Eventually, one of the five dogs on line would retrieve the bird.

Skipper Bob, whose progeny were mated so often with Prince, was adept at this type of test. Many times he would wait patiently on line while two or even three dogs were sent after the cripple. When his number finally was called, he would run out confidently to where the bird was last seen, track it diligently, and more times than not, return with it in his mouth.

"Wiping the eye" was the term used in those early days when the second, third, or fourth dog found the bird, and Skipper Bob excelled at this. In fact, in all of my research, Bob appears to be one of the best dogs in Chesapeake history for marking the location of the bird—and probably one of the best of all of the Retriever breeds. In other words, Chesapeakes are very good at marking birds.

Imagine, if you can, a cold, blustery day with five big Retrievers sitting patiently on line, and a single duck shot into high marshland. First the Labrador is sent. He fails and is picked up. Next the Golden goes. After a long hunt he also is picked up. Now Skipper Bob goes. Confidently and quickly, he goes to the area where the bird fell. (Remember, this is probably ten or twenty minutes after the actual fall.) He sniffs around thoroughly and then suddenly takes off at a tangent. Several minutes later a triumphant shout arises from the gallery. There is Bob with the big duck firmly held in his mouth. Again he has "wiped the eye" of his opponents. This is the Chesapeake.

A Chesapeake was first registered in the United States in 1878. His name was Sunday and he was owned by G. W. Kierstead of La Porte, Indiana. Whelped in 1875, Sunday was bred by O. D. Foulkes.

By 1934 almost half of the total Retrievers registered were Chesapeakes: 103 Chesapeakes out of a total of 283 Retrievers. In 1940 there were over one thousand registered Retrievers, with the Chesapeakes still representing more than one-third of the total. By 1945 Chesapeake registrations totaled 427. Registrations of the other two popular Retriever breeds had increased dramatically, and the Chesapeake was in third place to stay.

The Canadian dog Bud Parker was responsible for many modern bench show champions and is also to be found in pedigrees of many field trial winners.

Although total registrations of Chesapeakes are far behind those of Labradors and Goldens, Chesapeakes are distributed well throughout different sections of the country.

On the East Coast the Daniel Horns have developed their Eastern Water strain, which excels in both show and obedience. And August and Louise Belmont maintained their South Bay Kennels on Long Island for many years, with dogs going back to Atom Bob. The Belmonts have since moved to Maryland and are out of Chesapeakes and into Labradors, which is a great loss to the Chesapeake fancy.

William Hoard, Jr., was quite active in the fifties and early sixties in producing dogs of the deadgrass color that went back to such great stock as Deerwood Trigger, a field trial and amateur field trial champion. The Deerwood strain has long been bred by P. J. Gagnon of Robbinsdale, Minnesota.

There are many others, such as Dr. John Lundy in the West, who produced Field Trial and Amateur Field Trial Champion Atom Bob, the sire of so many good field dogs. And so it goes. In subsequent chapters you will read more about these and many other Chesapeakes who have contributed to this great hunting breed.

Above: Brush, a celebrated Retriever, from a painting by A. Cooper, R.A., pictured in *The Dog Book*, by Jam Watson, 1906.

Above: Bonnacord Darkie, a Retriever owned by Mr. R. T. Baines, Urmston, Manchester, England. From *The Dog Book*, by James Watson, 1906.

Below: Early Retriever, photographed by C. Reid, Wishaw. From *The New Book of the Dog*, by Robert Leighton, 1911.

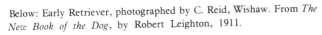

Below: Erin's Float, an Irish Water Spaniel described as particularly good in head and face. Property of Reverend T. Moore Smith, Scotch Plains, New Jersey. From *The Dog Book*, by James Watson, 1906.

"Water Dog," by P. Reinagle, R.A. Originally appearing in *The Sportsman's Cabinet*, published in 1803, this illustration is reproduced from *The New Book of the Dog*, by Robert Leighton, published in 1911.

Below, Gammon Gata, Chesapeake Bay Dog, owned by Mr. A. M. Coghlin, Toledo, Ohio. From *The Dog Book*, by James Watson, 1906. This Retriever and the one pictured above are similar in type to the probable progenitors of the Chesapeake Bay Retriever.

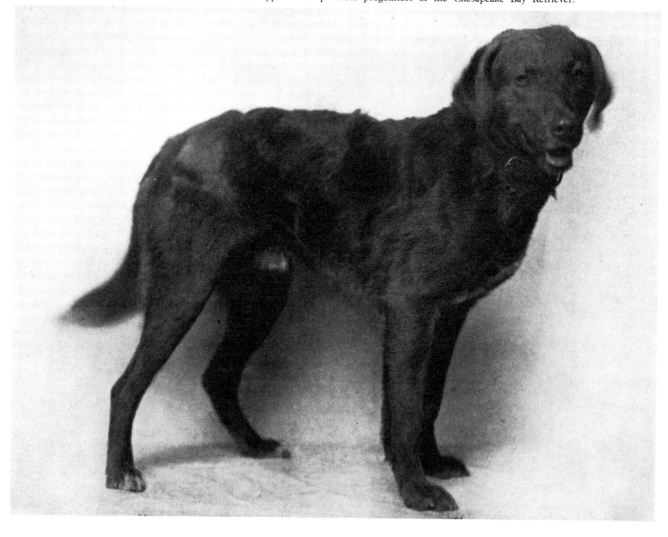

How the Chesapeake Bay Retriever Differs From Other Retriever Breeds

This might sound like trivia to many readers, but, believe me, there are basic and important differences in the Retriever breeds.

Many people are of the opinion that all dogs are retrievers at heart and that all they need is the training. This just is not true. Let me illustrate. Some time back, an acquaintance of mine who raised and trained German Shepherds came down to watch one of our "fun" trials. After observing the Derby series carefully, he announced to all and sundry that he easily could train one of his young Shepherds to do as well as the Retrievers, or better. Since I had a few Derby dogs in training, I "reluctantly" made a small wager with him and then spent the next few months deciding how I was going to spend the money.

At our next "fun" trial, my friend showed up eagerly with his Shepherd in tow. The dog was docile, well trained in obedience, and he heeled well up to the line. That was the end of it.

The first test was a simple water double retrieve with shackled ducks, one thrown from a point about fifty yards out and the other thrown right out in front of the dog with guns on each side. My two Labs, a Golden, and my Chesapeake completed the test with no trouble—and then came the Shepherd. When the far bird was thrown, he looked out intently, but when the two guns were fired, one from each side of him, he broke and ran. Where? Back to his crate in my friend's station wagon, and my friend couldn't get the Shepherd out again during the trial. My friend paid up gracefully but I never again saw him at a Retriever trial.

The foregoing was just to point out that not all dogs are able to retrieve, nor can all dogs be trained to retrieve as well as the various Retriever breeds. In the same sense, all Retriever breeds cannot be bulked together and treated as one, as many uninformed people are likely to do. In many respects, the Retriever breeds are as different from one another as day is from night.

Today's Chesapeake has a distinct personality—one that was evolved way back in the early part of the twentieth century when the Chesapeake was used primarily as a "meat" dog. By that I mean that market hunters, men who killed their ducks for a living, were the main hunters and there were almost no rules and regulations controlling them.

These hunters usually would use a 10 gauge magnum with a scatter barrel, bringing down as many as fifty or sixty birds with one shot. If the hunter surprised a large flock on the water, there could easily be over a hundred casualties. Now, the market hunter wanted those birds for resale, and he usually had a Chesapeake to retrieve the birds for him. The Chessie had the sense to bring in the wounded birds before the dead ones. He would work tirelessly and steadily over a long, cold, ten or twelve hour day, as long as he could see to retrieve and his master could see to shoot.

Many of these market hunters lived in shacks, alone, along the bay or river that they hunted. If the hunter went into town in the evening for a libation or two, it was his Retriever's job to guard his shack and his birds against any intruder, man or beast. The Chesapeake also was far better than the other Retriever breeds for this. Many of the Chesapeakes of that era were loners, obeying only one person and trusting no one else, but superb at their job.

Now we approach the 1930s when field trials for Retrievers made their debut. The Chesapeakes were still prominent, but this was a different kettle of fish. The Chessie now had to be a gentleman.

Four or five dogs were on line simultaneously, with one working and the others looking on. This called for restraint on the part of the honoring dogs. Many of the Chesapeakes had tempers, but they took the training well. This, however, did not usually apply to kenneling together. The Labrador, the gentleman's shooting dog, had arrived on the scene and was making inroads. While Labradors could be turned loose in a large run for exercise, I would hesitate to try that with Chesapeakes. This is one basic difference in two of the Retriever breeds. Golden Retrievers also can be run together, assuming that they are trained. I have tried this with Irish Water Spaniels, but they did not do well together, in one pen. Not even a dog and bitch. This was some thirty years ago, though, and I understand the breed has changed.

The Chesapeake has a completely different character from that of the other Retriever breeds. If a Chesapeake is raised by a family for a year, he usually will not adjust to new surroundings easily. He is basically a one-man or one-family dog. This is in direct contrast to the Golden Retriever, who will move from one set of surroundings to another with complete equanimity. One time we had reason to place a nine-year-old Golden Retriever who was a trained hunting dog. He went cheerfully with his new owners, and when we visited, he acknowledged our presence with a mere wag of his tail.

The Labrador is not that placid, but neither is he as devoted as the Chesapeake.

In trials Labradors usually will do better for people who have trained them than they will for their owners, but Chesapeakes usually work better for their owners.

My top Labrador, for instance, used to break for me at almost half of his trials, but he never broke once when another professional handler ran him.

At home, the Chesapeake makes a very good house dog. He does not have a peculiar odor, as some novices state, although his coat might be a bit odoriferous when wet. And the Chesapeake—at least mine—is almost always wet. If there is ice on the water, he breaks it. If it's too hard to break, he will roll in the snow or do something else to dampen his coat. Perhaps this is where the aforementioned misconception concerning odor originates.

Besides being a good companion for you and your family, the Chesapeake also furnishes superior protection. The only thing a Chessie fears is loss of his master's affection. I often have stated that I would sooner walk unannounced into a house where there was a Doberman on guard than one where there was a Chesapeake.

The other Retriever breeds are so-so in this respect. Some Labradors offer protection, but almost no Golden Retrievers do—besides barking, that is. The Irish Water Spaniel used to be tough, but, to my knowledge, there are none of that particular ilk left around.

As for cleanliness in the house, the Golden Retriever is house trained the most easily, the Chesapeake ranks next, and the Labrador last. Many of my Labs would make a mistake in my house if they were left in just a short time beyond their usual span. Normally, Goldens house train at three months. The Chessie is in between.

All of the three main Retriever breeds should be trained young, but this is much more important for the Chesapeake than the other two. If your Chesapeake shows a pugnacious attitude at an early age, he must be corrected—vigorously and firmly.

Our latest pup, at the age of eight weeks, took to guarding his food dish and would snap at anyone or anything that went near him while he was eating. He tried this once with my wife, but she picked him up and slapped him sharply across the muzzle, and that is all that was needed for him to see that this kind of conduct would only bring him grief, so he stopped. I might add that a rolled-up newspaper usually won't make any impression on a Chesapeake. You really have to be firm. One thing is certain, though—once the Chesapeake learns, he doesn't forget, while the other breeds tend to.

To sum it all up, I have had many Chesapeakes, many Goldens, and many Labradors, as well as four very tough Irish Water Spaniels many years ago. But for an all-round show dog, guard dog, hunter, companion, and anything else you can think of, I would choose the Chesapeake, although I have many pleasant memories of the other Retriever breeds.

Mount Joy's Mallard, the first Dual Champion and Amateur Field Champion in the Chesapeake breed. Bred by Bob Brown and owned by Ed and Helen Fleischmann.

The Standard of the Breed

A breed Standard is a detailed written description of the perfect specimen of a breed. Written by breeders and owners and adopted by the breed club, the Standard is based on carefully kept breeding records, litter registration records, studbook data, and records concerning the history and evolution of the breed. Formulation of the Standard is the first step taken in gaining American Kennel Club recognition for a breed, and at the time the breed is recognized, the Standard of the breed is formally approved by The American Kennel Club.

In the conformation show ring, judges compare the individual dogs with the description in the Standard. Since there is no all-round perfect specimen in any breed, a judge evaluates the good qualities and poor qualities of each dog being shown, weighs the good qualities of the dog against its poor qualities, and thus selects the best specimens of a breed in a particular show on a particular day.

Breeders use the official description in the Standard in determining the quality of the dogs they include in their breeding programs. In selecting breeding stock, breeders follow a procedure similar to that of the dog show judges. But in order to produce the best possible offspring, a breeder must also consider how the qualities of one particular dog may complement those of another dog which is to be its mate.

Individual interpretations of a Standard may vary somewhat, but, basically, all judges, breeders, and breed owners are looking for the same thing: an all-round fine specimen of the particular breed.

Ideas of breed excellence change from time to time, bringing about evolutionary changes in a breed. Hence, Standards may be rewritten or revised occasionally. The original Standard of the Chesapeake Bay Retriever was adopted by The American Chesapeake Club on July 1, 1933. It was approved by The American Kennel Club on September 12 of that same year. In August 1963, the Standard was amended slightly, and it was amended again on November 9, 1976. All of the amendments are included here.

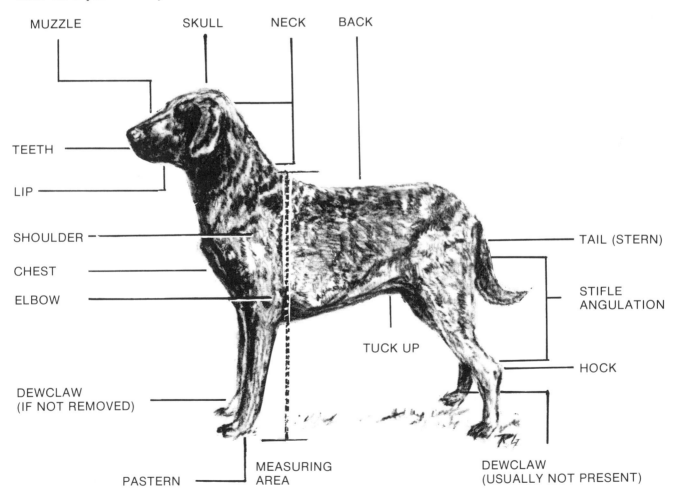

MUZZLE   SKULL   NECK   BACK

TEETH

LIP

SHOULDER

CHEST

ELBOW

DEWCLAW (IF NOT REMOVED)

PASTERN   MEASURING AREA

TUCK UP

TAIL (STERN)

STIFLE ANGULATION

HOCK

DEWCLAW (USUALLY NOT PRESENT)

The Standard of the Chesapeake Bay Retriever

Head—Skull broad and round with medium stop, nose medium to short, muzzle pointed but not sharp. Lips thin, not pendulous. Ears small, set well up on head, hanging loosely and of medium leather. Eyes medium large, very clear, of yellowish or amber color and wide apart.

Neck—of medium length with a strong muscular appearance, tapering to shoulders.

Shoulders, Chest and Body—Shoulders, sloping and should have full liberty of action with plenty of power without any restrictions of movement. Chest strong, deep and wide. Barrel round and deep. Body of medium length, neither cobby nor roached, but rather approaching hollowness, flanks well tucked up.

Hindquarters and Stifles—Hindquarters should be as high or a trifle higher than the shoulders. They should show fully as much power as the forequarters. There should be no tendency to weakness in either fore or hindquarters. Hindquarters should be especially powerful to supply the driving power for swimming. Back should be short, well-coupled and powerful. Good hindquarters are essential. Stifles should be well-angulated.

Legs, Elbows, Hocks and Feet—Legs should be medium length and straight, showing good bone and muscle, with well-webbed hare feet of good size. The toes well rounded and close, pasterns slightly bent and both pasterns and hocks medium length—the straighter the legs the better, when viewed from front or rear. Dewclaws, if any, must be removed from the hind legs. Dewclaws on the forelegs may be removed. A dog with dewclaws on the hind legs must be disqualified.

Tail—Tail should extend to hock. It should be medium heavy at base. Moderate feathering on stern and tail is permissible. Tail should be straight or slightly curved. Tail should not curl over back or side kink.

Coat and Texture—Coat should be thick and short, nowhere over 1½ inches long, with a dense fine wooly undercoat. Hair on face and legs should be very short and straight with tendency to wave on the shoulders, neck, back and loins only. The curly coat or coat with a tendency to curl not permissible.

The texture of the dog's coat is very important, as the dog is used for hunting under all sorts of adverse weather conditions, often working in ice and snow. The oil in the harsh outercoat and wooly undercoat is of extreme value in preventing the cold water from reaching the dog's skin and aids in quick drying. A Chesapeake's coat should resist the water in the same way that a duck's feathers do. When he leaves the water and shakes himself, his coat should not hold the water at all, being merely moist. Color and coat are extremely important, as the dog is used for duck hunting. The color must be as nearly that of his surroundings as possible and with the fact that dogs are exposed to all sorts of adverse weather conditions, often working in ice and snow, the color of the coat and its texture must be given every consideration when judging on the bench or in the ring.

Color—Any color varying from a dark brown to a faded tan or deadgrass. Deadgrass takes in any shade of deadgrass, varying from a tan to a dull straw color. White spot on breast, toes and belly is permissible, but the smaller the spot the better. Solid and self-colored dogs are preferred.

Weight—Males, 65 to 80 pounds; females, 55 to 70 pounds.

Height—Males, 23 inches to 26 inches; females, 21 inches to 24 inches. Oversized or undersized dogs are to be severely penalized.

Symmetry and Quality—The Chesapeake dog should show a bright and happy disposition and an intelligent expression, with general outlines impressive and denoting a good worker. The dog should be well proportioned, a dog with a good coat and well balanced in other points being preferable to the dog excelling in some but weak in others.

Courage, willingness to work, alertness, nose, intelligence, love of water, general quality, and, most of all, disposition, should be given primary consideration in the selection and breeding of the Chesapeake Bay dog.

POSITIVE SCALE OF POINTS

Head, incl. lips, ears & eyes	16
Neck	4
Shoulders and body	12
Hindquarters and stifles	12
Elbows, legs and feet	12
Color	4
Stern and tail	10
Coat and texture	18
General conformation	12
TOTAL	100

NOTE: The question of coat and general type of balance takes precedence over any scoring table which could be drawn up.

APPROXIMATE MEASUREMENTS

	Inches
Length head, nose to occiput	9½ to 10
Girth at ears	20 to 21
Muzzle below eyes	10 to 10½
Length of ears	4½ to 5
Width between eyes	2½ to 2¾
Girth neck close to shoulder	20 to 22
Girth at flank	24 to 25
Length from occiput to tail base	34 to 35
Girth forearms at shoulders	10 to 10½
Girth upper thigh	19 to 20
From root to root of ear, over skull	5 to 6
Occiput to top shoulder blades	9 to 9½
From elbow to elbow over the shoulders	25 to 26

DISQUALIFICATIONS

Black.
Dewclaws on hind legs.
White on any part of body, except breast, belly or spots on feet.
Feathering on tail or legs over 1¼ inches long.
Undershot, overshot or any deformity.
Coat curly or tendency to curl all over body.
Specimens unworthy or lacking in breed characteristics.
Approved November 9, 1976

Interpretation of the Standard

Here we shall discuss the more important points of the Chesapeake Standard and explain what is meant by them.

In considering the head, the most important points are the muzzle and the bite, for the Chesapeake is expected to pick up large ducks and geese that often are alive and still struggling. The muzzle should be pointed but not sharp and should have sufficient width that the dog can grasp a large bird firmly in his mouth. The skull should be broad and round, so as to conform with the rest of the head. Now let us consider the bite. If the jaw is undershot, the bottom teeth will protrude beyond the upper teeth. This will interfere with the dog's picking up a bird properly. It is a disqualification in the show ring (as is the overshot jaw). Besides, if a dog with an undershot jaw is used for breeding, at least some of the progeny will inherit the characteristic. The same is true of an overshot jaw, where the upper jaw and teeth protrude over the lower. This also is a great impediment to the dog's picking up a bird and also is hereditary.

Next in importance are the neck and shoulders. The neck should be of moderate length, and powerful—again to enable the dog to handle large birds properly. The shoulders supply a major part of the powerful drive the Chesapeake has, both when running and swimming, but particularly when swimming. The shoulders should slope with full liberty of action and plenty of power, and without restriction of movement.

The chest must be strong, deep, and wide to accommodate the lungs which the Chesapeake needs for swimming long distances.

When it comes to the back quarters and stifles, even the novice can see the relationship of back to front. Back quarters should be as high as if not a trifle higher than the shoulders and should show fully as much power as the forequarters. (While I can agree with this point, I cannot see how the Chesapeake can also be well angulated, but this is the way the Standard is written.)

Hindquarters should be especially powerful to supply the driving power for swimming. To understand this, there is no substitute for actually observing a Chesapeake swimming after something, especially in clear water. The tuck up of the flank as described in the Standard is quite noticeable in photos of Chesapeakes in the field but is much less noticeable in show dogs. Remember that the back should be short, well coupled, and powerful, for these characteristics are also basic requirements for water work.

An important disqualification in the Chesapeake Standard is the presence of dewclaws on the rear legs. A dewclaw is the so-called fifth toe, usually high up on the foot and with a claw that protrudes. Dewclaws occur on both front and rear legs. While dewclaws on the rear legs disqualify a Chesapeake from competition, the Standard states that dewclaws on the front legs *may* be removed. In my opinion, all dewclaws should be removed, for they are a definite impediment, especially when the dog is moving through marshes or through ice or snow.

Next in importance in the Chesapeake Standard is the coat. It should be thick and short, with a dense, fine, wooly undercoat. The coat should also be oily, for a good Chesapeake coat will shed water much as a duck's feathers do. If, when examining a coat, the judge were to run his hand against the lie of the hair and find little or no undercoat, the dog would be penalized severely because it obviously could not do its job in the water without freezing to death. On the other hand, if at dog shows it were mandatory that a dog be examined while it is "wet," then running the hand against the lie of the hair of a good Chesapeake should expose an almost dry undercoat.

Much is made of the coat color and of the Chesapeake's blending into its surroundings while hunting. I have seen too many ducks decoy in to every color of dog, especially black, to place much credence in this stipulation in the Standard. Nevertheless, it is there, and if you are judging, you must adhere to it.

In 1976, The American Chesapeake Club added to the Standard the statement that self colored dogs are preferred. In the AKC glossary of terms, self colored is defined as one color or whole color except for lighter shadings. Yet black is a disqualification in Chesapeakes. (You figure that one out.)

The Chesapeake should show a bright and happy disposition and an intelligent expression. These important characteristics should be apparent in puppies, in Chesapeakes that are working, and in Chesapeakes that are being exhibited in the show ring. Always look for a wagging tail, a happy expression, and boldness and aggressiveness. In the older dog, look especially for courage, both when the dog is retrieving on land and when he is retrieving in the water. Courage is a sign of good breeding and good temperament.

The largest number of points, eighteen, is given to coat and texture, bringing out once again the importance of the coat. Color is given only four points. Again, this is as it should be, for any solid color from dark brown to a faded tan or deadgrass is acceptable.

To sum up the requirements, the overall structure of the jaw should be wide enough and large enough to handle a large mallard or a Canada goose with ease. And the neck and shoulder muscles should be of great strength to carry these large birds. But the texture and quality of the coat and general balance of the Chesapeake overall must be considered more important than any other qualities.

A bird down. The "Bay dog" starting out to retrieve

Turning back to shore in good form

The dog, the bird, the man and the decoys—all in one picture

Bringing in the bird

The dog's share of the sport

Delivering the bird

THE CHESAPEAKE BAY DOG AT WORK

From *The Dog Book*, by James Watson, 1906.

16

Field Trials

What is a field trial? The American Kennel Club (AKC) defines a field trial as "a competition for certain Hound or Sporting Breeds in which dogs are judged on ability and style in finding or retrieving game or following a game trail."

The Chessie is, of course, classed as a Sporting Breed and may compete in field trials which are governed by The American Kennel Club *Rules for Retriever Trials.* Amplification of these rules is provided in the *Standard Procedure for Non-Slip Retriever Trials.*

What is a Non-Slip Retriever? The AKC defines a Non-Slip Retriever as a dog "that walks at heel, marks the fall, and retrieves game on command; not expected to find or flush." That statement tells quite succinctly what is expected of the Chesapeake, both as a field trial dog and in hunting game.

In addition to competing under the AKC rules governing field trials, Chessies (if qualified) may also run in local and/or national events accredited under the American Field Association, Field Dog Stud Book, which also registers dogs and records results of organized trials which it accredits. Points from these trials, however, do not apply toward AKC championships.

The AKC *Rules for Retriever Trials* and the *Standard Procedure for Non-Slip Retriever Trials,* which follow, provide the answers to all the questions any Chessie owner may have about the various types of stakes in which the Chessie may compete, just what is expected of the Chessie in each type of stake, and how the Chessie may earn points toward his AKC field championship.

Three generations: Field Champion and Amateur Field Champion Atom Bob with Dr. John C. Lundy; Champion and Amateur Field Champion Bomarc of South Bay, C.D. (Bob's son), with August Belmont; and South Bay Nike (Bomarc's daughter), with Louise Belmont. Photo taken at the Club's Specialty Trial in Boise, Idaho, in May 1963.

RULES FOR RETRIEVER TRIALS

SECTION 1. Wherever used in this chapter and in the Standard Procedure for Non-Slip Retriever Trials, the word Retriever shall be deemed to include the several breeds of Retrievers and/or Irish Water Spaniels.

Field trial clubs or specialty clubs formed for the improvement of any one of the several breeds of Retrievers may give field trial stakes in which one of said breeds only may compete, or in which more than one of said breeds may compete together.

Championship points may be awarded where two or more of said breeds compete together in a mixed stake as well as where a separate stake has been provided for each breed.

SECTION 2. Only pure-bred Retrievers over six months of age may be entered in field trials.

The owner or agent entering a dog in a trial does so at his own risk, and agrees to abide by the Rules of The American Kennel Club.

A dog is not eligible to be entered or to compete in any licensed or member trial in any stake, if a Judge of that stake or any member of his family has owned, sold, held under lease, boarded (except as a veterinarian incidental to veterinary care), or trained the dog, or handled the dog at more than two trials, within one year prior to the starting date of the field trial, or if a Judge or any member of his family holds a direct financial interest contingent upon the dog's performance.

No post entries will be accepted and entries shall close not later than the time of the drawing, which drawing shall take place at least three days before the first day of the trial.

Judges shall have the power to disqualify any dog which shall not appear within fifteen minutes of the time designated for its turn to be tried.

Bitches in season shall not be eligible for competition in any stake and shall not be allowed on the field trial grounds. The entry fees of bitches withdrawn because of coming in season shall be refunded.

Judges shall have the power to exclude from competition any dog which the Judges may consider unfit to compete. The entry fee of all such dogs will be forfeited.

A dog is not eligible to be entered or to compete in any licensed or member trial in any stake if the dog has on three occasions been made the subject of the following report: If a dog, while under judgment, attacks another dog, and if the Judges are unanimously of the opinion that such attack was without reasonable cause, the Judges shall identify the offending dog on the judging sheet and the name of the offending dog shall be listed in the report of the trial sent to The American Kennel Club.

SECTION 3. Only Amateurs shall be asked to judge licensed or member Retriever Trials. In Stakes carryng championship points

there shall be only two Judges, and their combined experience should conform to the provisions set forth in Section 23 of the Standard Procedure.

SECTION 4. In Stakes for Retrievers the order of running shall be decided by lot at the draw, dogs worked by the same person or belonging to the same owner being separated when possible. At the option of the trial-giving club the drawing may be arranged so that all bitches are drawn after all dogs.

Dogs may be run in an order different from the order in which they are drawn:

(a) When in the opinion of the Judges or the Field Trial Committee such will result in a reasonable and desirable saving of time in the conduct of the trial, or

(b) When in the opinion of the Judges such will avoid unfairness or prejudice to any competing dog resulting from an event which has occurred in the particular stake, or

(c) Beginning after the first series, in a stake carrying championship points, when the Judges have been authorized by the trial-giving club to impose a system of rotation which applies to all contestants. The authorization must be stated in the Premium List. Rotation may not be employed in a stake in which all bitches are drawn after all dogs.

SECTION 5. Only stakes which are run on game birds and on both land and water shall be permitted to carry championship points. Premium lists should specify the kind of game to be used in each stake, and, unless otherwise specified in the premium list, only pheasants and ducks may be used in stakes carrying championship points, and pheasants or pigeons and ducks in other stakes.

SECTION 6. After a Field Trial Committee has selected field trial grounds, no competing dog shall be trained on that part of the grounds to be used for the trial.

SECTION 7. In the event of the weather proving unsuitable for holding the trials, the Field Trial Committee may suspend or postpone any or all stakes up to three days. Notice of such postponement shall be forwarded immediately to The American Kennel Club.

Postponement beyond three days must have the approval of The American Kennel Club.

In the event of postponement of 24 hours or more in the starting time of any stake, any competitor shall have the right to withdraw his entries and his entry fees shall be returned to him.

SECTION 8. Splitting of prizes and/or places at a Retriever Trial is prohibited. No cash or merchandise shall be given as prizes for placing dogs. There shall be no prizes or trophies of any kind offered to handlers in any stake, except (a) trophies to Amateur Handlers and (b) a trophy to the handler of the winning dog in the National Championship Stake.

And away we go! Eloise Cherry sending Field Champion, Amateur Field Champion, and Canadian Field Champion Nelgard's Baron, C.D.

SECTION 9. The regular official stakes at a Retriever Trial shall be Derby, Qualifying, Open All-Age, Limited All-Age, Special All-Age and Amateur All-Age.

SECTION 10. A Derby Stake at a Retriever Trial shall be for dogs which have not reached their second birthday on the first day of the trial at which they are being run. For example, a dog whelped May 1, 1965, would not be eligible for Derby Stakes at a trial starting May 1, 1967, but would be eligible at a trial the first day of which was April 30, 1967.

A Qualifying Stake at a Retriever Trial shall be for dogs which have never won first, second, third or fourth place or a Judges' Award of Merit in an Open All-Age, Limited All-Age or Special All-Age Stake, or won first, second, third or fourth place in an Amateur All-Age Stake, or won two first places in Qualifying Stakes at licensed or member club trials. In determining whether a dog is eligible for the Qualifying Stake, no award received on or after the date of closing of entries shall be counted.

An Open All-Age Stake at a Retriever Trial shall be for all dogs.

A Limited All-Age Stake at a Retriever Trial shall be for dogs that have previously been placed or awarded a Judges' Award of Merit in an Open All-Age Stake or Amateur All-Age Stake carrying championship points in each case, or that have been placed first or second in a Qualifying Stake.

A Special All-Age Stake at a Retriever Trial shall be for dogs that, during the period comprised of the previous calendar year and the current calendar year prior to the date of closing of entries for such trial, have been placed or awarded a Judges' Award of Merit in an Open All-Age Stake. Limited All-Age Stake, Special All-Age Stake or Amateur All-Age Stake, carrying championship points in each case, or have been placed first or second in a Qualifying Stake.

An Amateur All-Age Stake at a Retriever Trial shall be for any dogs, if handled in that stake by persons who are Amateurs (as determined by the Field Trial Committee of the trial-giving club).

SECTION 11. At any field trial, there shall not be more than one of the following stakes: Open All-Age, Limited All-Age or Special All-Age and no club shall hold more than two of such stakes in one calendar year.

In a two-day trial, when one of the above stakes is held, not more than two other stakes shall be held unless more than one stake is run at the same time under different Judges.

SECTION 12. A National Championship Stake for qualified Retrievers shall be run not more than once in any calendar year by the National Retriever Club under the Rules and Procedures of Retriever Trials subject to such modifications of these Rules and Procedures as may be considered necessary by the National Retriever Club. The club may also make special Rules and Procedures as are deemed necessary for the conduct of the stake. Modifications of the Rules and Procedures as well as such special Rules and Procedures as may be made by the National Retriever Club, are subject to the approval of the Board of Directors of The American Kennel Club. The winner of such stake shall become a Field Champion of Record if registered in The American Kennel Club Stud Book and shall be entitled to be designated "National Retriever Field Champion of 19--."

SECTION 13. A National Amateur Championship Stake for qualified Retrievers shall be run not more than once in any calendar year by the National Amateur Retriever Club under the Rules and Procedures for Retriever trials subject to such modifications of these Rules and Procedures as may be considered necessary by the National Amateur Retriever Club. The club may also make special Rules and Procedures as are deemed necessary for the conduct of the stake. Modifications of the Rules and Procedures as well as such special Rules and Procedures as may be made by the National Amateur Retriever Club, are subject to the approval of the Board of Directors of The American Kennel Club. The winner of such stake shall become an Amateur Field Champion of Record if registered in The American

Kennel Club Stud Book and shall be entitled to be designated "National Amateur Retriever Field Champion of 19--."

SECTION 14. Non-regular stakes may be held at Retriever Trials subject to the approval of The American Kennel Club, and provided the premium list sets forth any special conditions regarding eligibility for entry, and any special conditions regarding the method of conducting or judging the stake. Such stakes will not carry championship points or be considered as qualifying a dog for any other stake.

SECTION 15. A Retriever shall become a Field Champion of Record, if registered in The American Kennel Club Stud Book, after having won points in Open All-Age, Limited All-Age or Special All-Age Stakes at field trials of member clubs of The American Kennel Club or at field trials of non-member clubs licensed by The American Kennel Club to hold field trials.

SECTION 16. A Retriever shall become an Amateur Field Champion of Record, if registered in The American Kennel Club Stud Book, after having won points in Open All-Age, Limited All-Age or Special All-Age Stakes when handled by an Amateur (as determined by the Field Trial Committee of the trial-giving club) and in Amateur All-Age Stakes at field trials of member clubs of The American Kennel Club or at trials of non-member clubs licensed by The American Kennel Club to hold trials.

SECTION 17. The total number of points required for a championship, the number of places in a stake for which points may be required, the number of points to be acquired for each place, and the number of starters required and their qualifications for eligibility to acquire points in each stake shall be fixed and determined by the Board of Directors of The American Kennel Club.

At each trial having an Open All-Age Stake, or an Amateur All-Age Stake, the Field Trial Secretary in his report must certify whether at least twelve (12) of the starters in each of those stakes were eligible to compete in a Limited All-Age Stake.

At each trial having an Open All-Age, Limited All-Age or Special All-Age Stake, the Field Trial Secretary in his report must specify which handlers of placing dogs, if any, in such stakes are determined to be Amateurs by their Field Trial Committee.

At present, to acquire an Amateur Field Championship, a Retriever must win:

(1) a National Championship Stake, handled by an Amateur, or a National Amateur Championship Stake or (2) a total of 10 points in Open All-Age, Limited All-Age, or Special All-Age Stakes or a total of 15 points in Open All-Age, Limited All-Age, Special All-Age, or Amateur All-Age Stakes, which may be acquired as follows: In each Open All-Age, Limited All-Age, Special All-Age, or Amateur All-Age Stake, there must be at least 12 starters, each of which is eligible for entry in a Limited All-Age Stake, and the handler must be an Amateur (as determined by the Field Trial Committee of the trial-giving club), and the winner of first place shall be credited with 5 points, second place 3 points, third place 1 point, and fourth place 1/2 point, but before acquiring a championship, a dog must win a first place and acquire 5 points in at least one Open All-Age, Limited All-Age, Special All-Age, or Amateur All-Age Stake open to all breeds of Retriever, and not more than 5 points shall be acquired in trials not open to all breeds of Retriever.

At present, to acquire a Field Championship, a Retriever must win:

(1) a National Championship Stake or (2) a total of 10 points, which may be acquired as follows: In each Open All-Age, Limited All-Age or Special All-Age Stake, there must be at least 12 starters, each of which is eligible for entry in a Limited All-Age Stake, and the winner of first place shall be credited with 5 points, second place 3 points, third place 1 point, and fourth place 1/2 point, but before acquiring a championship a dog must win first place and acquire 5 points in at least one Open All-Age, Limited All-Age, or Special All-Age Stake open to all breeds of Retriever, and not more than 5 points of the required 10 shall be acquired in trials not open to all breeds of Retriever.

STANDARD PROCEDURE FOR NON-SLIP RETRIEVER TRIALS

In order that trials may be conducted as uniformly as practicable, standardization of objectives is essential and, therefore, all Judges, Guns, contestants and officials who have a part in conducting trials should be familiar with and be governed so far as possible by the following standard:

BASIC PRINCIPALS

1. The purpose of a Non-Slip Retriever Trial is to determine the relative merits of Retrievers in the field. Retriever field trials should, therefore, simulate as nearly as possible the conditions met in an ordinary day's shoot.

Dogs are expected to retrieve any type of game bird under all conditions, and the Judges and the Field Trial Committee have complete control over the mechanics and requirements of each trial. This latitude is permitted in order to allow for the difference in conditions which may arise in trials given in widely separated parts of the United States, which difference well may necessitate different methods of conducting tests.

2. The function of a Non-Slip Retriever is to seek and retrieve "fallen" game when ordered to do so. He should sit quietly on line or in the blind, walk at heel, or assume any station designated by his handler until sent to retrieve. When ordered, a dog should retrieve quickly and briskly without unduly disturbing too much ground, and should deliver tenderly to hand. He should then await further orders.

Accurate marking is of primary importance. A dog which marks the fall of a bird, uses the wind, follows a strong cripple, and will take direction from his handler is of great value.

TRIAL PROCEDURE

3. The Judges, with due regard to the recommendations of the Field Trial Committee, shall determine the tests to be given in each series— and shall try to give all dogs approximately similar tests in the same series. The Judges may discontinue any test before it has been completed, provided that another test is substituted therefor. The performance of a dog in a test which has been discontinued shall not be considered for any purpose in the evaluation of the work of that dog in the stake.

4. At the end of the first series, and every series thereafter, the Judges will call back all dogs which they wish to try further, and will cause them to run in additional series until the stake is decided.

5. Judges shall in their discretion determine the number of dogs that shall be worked or kept on line simultaneously. In at least one test involving the retrieve of a marked fall in all stakes, except Derby, every dog should be kept on line off leash while another dog works.

6. When coming to line to be tested, and while on line, the dog and handler should assume such positions as may be directed by the Judges.

Dogs should be considered under judgment from the time they are called to come to the line until they have left the line and are back of all the Judges and on leash.

Leashes and collars shall be used as follows:

(a) In stakes carrying championship points, dogs shall be brought to the line and taken from the line off leash and without collar while under judgment; in these stakes collars and leashes may be put on the dogs after they leave the line and are in back of all the Judges.

(b) in Qualifying Stakes the procedure should be the same as in stakes carrying championship points except:

(i) Dogs shall be brought to and taken from the line on leash and wearing collars if all handlers are instructed by the Judges to do so, and

(ii) when handlers are instructed to pick up dogs because of missed birds or other conditions under which the dogs are expected to return on the line, collars or leashes may at once be put on dogs on line.

(c) In Derby Stakes, solely at the handler's option, dogs may wear collars while under judgment and may be brought to the line and taken from the line on leash or off leash—the leash being removed from the time of arrival on line until departure.

No dog should run with bandages or tape of any kind without the approval of the Field Trial Committee. The Committee should inspect the injury for which the bandage or tape is being used unless, of their own knowledge, they already possess such information, or unless they are furnished with a veterinary's certificate setting forth this information to their satisfaction.

7. The dogs should be shot over by Guns appointed by the Field Trial Committee.

8. On marked retrieves, a dog should be able to see each bird in the air and as it falls, and the Guns should be so stationed as to be conspicuous to and easily identified by the dog. Guns may be requested to shoot twice at every bird. After birds have been shot, all Guns shall remain quietly and only move their positions in accordance with specific instructions by Judges. Judges may request Guns to disappear from sight after their bird is down, but they should not have them move to another position to deliberately mislead the dogs in their marking. On marked retrieves the order in which birds are to be retrieved shall not be specified by the Judges. The handler is free to select the order in which he directs his dog to retrieve the birds provided that such selection should be accomplished quietly and promptly.

9. When possible in land series, game should be dropped on fresh territory for each dog and not on ground already fouled.

10. When on line, a handler should not place his dog or himself so that the dog's full vision of any birds or falls is blocked. This applies to the working dog and the honoring dog. Violation of this provision, if determined by the Judges to be deliberate, is sufficient cause to justify elimination from the stake.

11. Unless otherwise instructed by the Judges, no dog should be sent to retrieve until his number has been called by one of the Judges.

12. Judges should call the number of the dog ordered to retrieve rather than the name of the handler or the dog.

13. If, when a dog is ordered by the Judge to retrieve a fall, another dog breaks for the same fall and interferes with the working dog to the extent of causing him in any way to make a faulty performance, the dog interfered with should be considered as not having been tried and given a chance for another performance.

14. If there is an occurrence which makes for a relatively unfair test for a dog, the Judges shall exercise their discretion in determining how to form a judgment of the quality of the work of the dog in the series notwithstanding the unfairness. In forming such judgment the Judges may decide that it is necessary or unnecessary to re-run the dog. If they decide the latter, they may waive delivery to hand of the mark or blind in which the unfairness occurred; if they decide the former, the dog shall be picked up immediately and tested on a new set of birds, if practicable, after waiting behind the line until several other dogs have been tested.

The re-run of a mark or blind which was not previously completed shall be scored by taking into consideration the combined performances of the dog prior to the point of unfairness in the initial run and after the point of unfairness in the re-run. If there shall be more than one re-run of that mark or blind, the Judges shall exercise their discretion in determining how to score it fairly.

The re-run of a mark or blind which was previously completed shall be scored on the first completion and faults committed on such re-run shall be ignored except that if the dog (1) does not complete that portion in accordance with the Judges' instructions for the test or (2) commits any of the faults set forth herein as usually justifying elimination from a stake, he shall be penalized in the same manner as the Judges would penalize him regardless of the re-run.

Notwithstanding the last sentence of Standard Procedure 8, a handler is not free to select marked falls in a re-run in an order different from the order in which they were selected in the initial run and if the handler deliberately attempts to do so the dog shall be eliminated from the stake.

15. When ordered to retrieve, the handler shall direct his dog from any position ordered by the Judges.

16. Retrievers should perform equally well on the land and in the water, and should be thoroughly tested on both.

17. During at least one water test in all stakes, dogs should be worked over artificial decoys, anchored separately.

18. Until called to be tested, a dog must be kept where it cannot see the location of a fall for another dog, or see the planting or retrieve of a blind, unless such be in compliance with instructions of the Judges as in a test in which the dog is required to honor before being run. Violation of this section shall cause the dog to be eliminated from the stake. If the Judges or the Field Trial Committee believe the violation to have been deliberate, the occurrence shall be deemed to have been a display of unsportsmanlike conduct by the handler and the penalties prescribed by Standard Procedure 38 shall also be applicable. If the incident occurs while the dog is under judgment the Judges shall decide whether or not there has been a violation of this section and whether or not it was deliberate, otherwise these decisions shall be made by the Field Trial Committee.

19. Nothing should be thrown to encourage a dog to enter the water or direct a dog to the fall. Violation of this provision is to be considered sufficient cause for elimination from the stake.

20. In stakes carrying championship points, there should be at least one handling test or blind retrieve—and preferably two, one on land and one in water.

21. Tests or retrieves which are not to be considered by the Judges at the final summing up should not be held.

JUDGING

Because of its concise statement of purpose, Section 2 of this Standard Procedure is repeated here:

2. The function of a Non-Slip Retriever is to seek and retrieve "fallen" game when ordered to do so. He should sit quietly on line or in the blind, walk at heel, or assume any station designated by his handler until sent to retrieve. When ordered, a dog should retrieve quickly and briskly without unduly disturbing too much ground, and should deliver tenderly to hand. He should then await further orders.

Accurate marking is of primary importance. A dog which marks the fall of a bird, uses the wind, follows a strong cripple, and will take direction from his handler is of great value.

22. The Judges must judge the dogs for (a) their natural abilities including their memory, intelligence, attention, nose, courage, perseverance and style, and (b) their abilities acquired through training, including steadiness, control, response to direction, and delivery. Decisions to eliminate a dog from a stake as a result of faulty performance must be the consensus of the Judges.

23. In stakes carrying championship points, the experience of the two Judges should be such that their combined experience includes the judging of 8 stakes carrying championship points.

LINE MANNERS

24. When called to be tested, a dog should come tractably at heel and sit promptly at the point designated by his handler and remain quietly where placed until given further orders. Retrievers which bark or whine on line, in a blind or while retrieving should be penalized. Loud and prolonged barking or whining is sufficient cause to justify elimination from the stake.

25. No handler shall (1) carry exposed any training equipment (except whistle) or use any other equipment or threatening gestures in such a manner that they may be an aid or threat in steadying or controlling a dog; (2) hold or touch a dog to keep him steady; or (3) noisily or frequently restrain a dog on line, except in extraordinary circumstances, from the time the first bird is being thrown until the dog's number is called. Violation of any of the provisions of this paragraph is sufficient cause to justify elimination from the stake.

A handler may, without penalty, give a command to sit as the first bird is thrown in a "walk-up." In other tests, during the period from the moment when, in accordance with the Judge's signal, the bird thrower commences his motion to throw the first bird until the dog's number is called, the handler of the working or honoring dog should remain silent. Also, in all marking tests, during such period, the handler's hands should remain quietly in close proximity to his body. A handler who projects his hand during such period, whether for the purpose of assisting his dog to locate a fall or otherwise, should be considered to have used a threatening gesture, and his dog penalized accordingly.

26. In an All-Age Stake, if a dog makes a movement which in the opinion of the Judges indicates a deliberate intent to retrieve without having been ordered to do so, that dog shall be deemed to have broken and shall be eliminated. In any stake other than an All-Age Stake, if a dog makes a slight break and is brought immediately under control, the dog need not be eliminated, but shall be penalized for unsteadiness.

If a dog on line creeps or jumps forward short of breaking as birds are shot and no effort is made by the handler to stop or restrain him, the Judges should not interpret such as a deliberate attempt to retrieve, since nothing was done to stop the dog. On the other hand, if the handler does make an effort to stop the dog, the Judges should assume that the handler believed the dog intended to retrieve and should deal with such infraction accordingly.

The Judges may require that dogs which have so jumped or crept forward be brought back to heel before being sent for their birds. A handler so ordered should bring his dog to a position satisfactory to the Judges and remain with him in such position until his number is called. In tests including honoring, care should be exercised to treat creeping, on the part of either dog, in a manner not grossly unfair to the other.

In all stakes, after the Judges have directed that a dog be ordered to retrieve, that dog is entitled to run in and retrieve and shall not be accused of, or penalized for breaking, even though the Judges did not see or hear the handler send the dog.

When a dog that is still in a stake, but not on line under judgment, breaks for a fall for a dog under judgment, in such a manner that the dog or his handler interferes, in the opinion of the Judges, with the normal conduct of the stake, that dog shall be eliminated from the stake.

When the handler of a dog under judgment is ordered by the Judges for any reason to pick up his dog, he is under judgment until he is back of all the Judges with his dog on leash, and all provisions of this section shall apply until that time.

27. After delivering a bird to his handler, a dog should stand or sit close to his handler until given further orders.

THE RETRIEVE

28. When ordered to retrieve, a dog should proceed quickly and eagerly on land or into the water to marked falls or on the line given him by his handler on falls he has not seen. He should not disturb too much ground or area and should respond quickly and obediently to any further directions his handler might give him. Failure to enter either rough cover, water, ice, mud or any other situation involving unpleasant or difficult going for the dog, after having been ordered to do so several times is sufficient cause to justify elimination from the stake.

A dog who pays no attention to many whistles and directions by his handler can be said to be "out-of-control," and unless in the opinion of the Judges there exist valid mitigating circumstances, should be eliminated from the stake.

29. In marking tests, a dog whose handler gives him a line in the direction of the fall, provided that such lining is accomplished briskly and precisely, should not by reason of such lining be outscored by a dog not so lined. However, conspicuously intensive lining is undesirable and should be penalized.

30. In marked retrieves, if a dog, after having been sent to retrieve, (1) returns to his handler before finding the bird, with or without having been called in, except in those cases of confusion of the dog as to whether he was really ordered to retrieve; (2) stops his hunt; or (3) fails to pick the bird up, actually leaving it after finding it, it shall be sufficient cause, unless there exist in the opinion of the Judges valid mitigating circumstances, to justify elimination from the stake.

31. A dog that goes to the area of a fall, hunts, fails to find and then leaves the area to hunt for another fall, or that drops a bird he is retrieving and goes for another, shall be considered to have "switched." Unless in the opinion of the Judges there exist valid mitigating circumstances, this fault constitutes sufficient justification for elimination from the stake.

32. A dog which fails to find a bird which, in the opinion of the Judges, he should have found, shall be eliminated from the stake.

33. Repeated evidence of poor nose is in itself sufficient justification for elimination from the stake. Because scenting conditions are affected by so many factors, Judges should exercise extreme caution in invoking this penalty.

34. A dog retrieving a decoy should be eliminated.

35. Upon finding the game, he should quickly pick it up and return briskly to his handler.

A dog should not drop his game on the ground, but distinction should be made between deliberately dropping a bird, and readjusting a bad hold of losing his grip because of a struggling bird or running over uneven terrain.

36. Upon returning, he should deliver the bird promptly and tenderly to his handler. A dog sitting to deliver should not outscore a dog making a clear delivery without sitting to do so. A dog that is unwilling to release a bird on delivery should be penalized, and if compelled to do so by severe methods should, unless in the opinion of the Judges there exist valid mitigating circumstances, be eliminated.

37. A dog should be eliminated for hard mouth or badly damaging game, but, before doing so, all Judges should inspect the bird and be satisfied that the dog alone was responsible for the damage.

Champion Cherokee's South Bay
Project, C.D., with a hen pheasant.

GENERAL

38. Any handler who displays unsportsmanlike conduct or who is seen to kick, strike or otherwise roughly manhandle a dog while on the grounds of a field trial at any time during the holding of a trial, may be expelled from competition in a stake, or from competition at the trial, by the Field Trial Committee.

It shall be the duty of the Committee to investigate, at once, any report that is made to it of alleged unsportsmanlike conduct on the part of a handler, or a report that a handler has been observed kicking, striking, or otherwise roughly manhandling a dog. If a Field Trial Committee, after investigation, determines that a handler is in violation of this section, it shall promptly notify the handler of its decision, specifying whether the handler is expelled from a particular stake or from further competition at the trials.

The Judges of a particular stake shall have the authority to expel a handler from any further competition in the stake, if they observe unsportsmanlike conduct on the part of the handler or see the handler kicking, striking, or otherwise roughly manhandling a dog while the judging of the stake is in progress. It will be the duty of the Judges to promptly report to the Field Trial Committee the expulsion of a handler from a stake and the Field Trial Committee may then expel the handler from all remaining competition at the trial, if in the Committee's opinion, such action is warranted.

Whenever a handler is expelled from a stake or from competition at a trial under this section, the dog or dogs that he is handling may continue in competition with one or more other handlers.

The Field Trial Secretary of a trial shall submit to The American Kennel Club, with the records of the trial, a report on any action taken under this section by either the Field Trial Committee or the Judges.

39. Judges shall have the power to turn out of the stake any dog which does not obey its handler and any handler who interferes willfully with another handler or his dog.

40. No dog shall be given a place in a stake unless the dog has competed in all tests held for any dog in such stake, except a test which has been discontinued.

41. The awarding of a Judges' Award of Merit to dogs which have passed every required test in a stake and have shown themselves to be well trained and qualified retrievers, should be encouraged.

GENERAL PROVISIONS

42. All field trial-giving clubs should clearly recognize that Open or Limited Stakes are of the first importance and that all other stakes are of relatively lesser importance, and are requested to adjust the timing of stakes so that time shall be available for a fair test in those stakes.

43. It is essential that all spectators attending a trial should be kept far enough from the line to enable the dog working to clearly discern his handler, and nothing shall be done to distract the dog's attention from his work. A handler has the right to appeal to the Judges if the gallery is interfering with his work in any way, and the Judges in their discretion may, if they believe the dog has been interfered with, give him another test.

44. There should be no practicing or training on any part of the field trial grounds from the start of the trial until its conclusion.

45. In sanctioned trials or non-regular stakes, any sections of this Standard Procedure may be relaxed or eliminated, but all contestants should be advised in what respects this is true.

The Chesapeake Bay Retriever Working Certificate

First, a word of explanation is in order. Just what is a Working Certificate? It is a certificate that is given when the Chesapeake performs correctly, certain tests set down by qualified judges under the rules of the American Chesapeake Club. The Working Certificate is meant primarily for dogs that usually do not compete in field trials and yet whose owners want people to know that the dog is a good retriever. This certificate also can be given by judges at a licensed trial when the dog performs creditably, even though he is not in the ribbons.

On Friday, April 6, 1973, the first American Chesapeake Club Working Dog Stake took place at Marshy Point, Maryland. Far from downgrading the working ability of the Chesapeake, the Working Certificate is often the only way of showing a dog's ability in this day of completely mechanized field trials and huge entries. In many cases this is the only evidence of "respectability" a Chessie has an opportunity to earn.

The Working Certificate tests for the Chesapeake are reasonable. They begin with two single retrieves on land. The first is a dead bird thrown into light cover, so it cannot be seen from the line. It should land about fifty yards out. The purpose of this is to determine whether the dog can mark (that is, note and remember where the bird fell), and if not, whether he will persevere and hunt for the bird. The second bird is a flyer (live bird) and is shot in a different area from that where the first was shot. The Guns are stationed about twenty yards from the line, and this second bird should also fall into light cover. This test is meant to determine whether or not the dog is gunshy and also will test his ability to handle freshly shot game.

The water tests are quite similar. Shackled ducks are used and two consecutive singles are thrown, each in a different area.

The prime reason for having the second retrieve is to see whether the Chessie will re-enter the water.

All of the foregoing is fine and dandy, but now comes a regulation that in my opinion makes this whole test just about useless. THE CHESAPEAKES ARE NOT REQUIRED TO BE STEADY. THEY MAY BE HELD ON LINE. This, in my opinion, is ludicrous. In almost all types of hunting and in field trials a Chessie should be steady, first and foremost. For jump shooting, hunting from blinds, or just plain waterfowl hunting, steadiness is the first requisite. I certainly wouldn't want some irresponsible dog tearing up the territory while I'm trying to shoot ducks, and I'm sure you wouldn't either.

Therefore, in my opinion, one of the more important rules in awarding Working Certificates would be to have the dog sit on line without making a move to retrieve while the birds are shot, and to go only when the judges tell the handler to send him. Thus would we take the measure of our Chesapeakes.

True, steadying the Chesapeake requires a lot more work than getting him ready for a dog show, but it can be done.

Despite this vagary, the Working Certificate is basically a step in the right direction. Any owner of a Retriever that obtains a Working Certificate by completing tests at a field trial can be especially proud. We have several that have done so—and all are steady.

Since I complained repeatedly about the requirements for the Chesapeake Working Certificate originated in 1973, and wrote several magazine articles about the lack of a requirement that the dog must be steady on line, the club has now initiated a W.D.X. (Working Dog Excellent) title which requires that the Chesapeake must be steady to shot without restraint for a double retrieve on land and water. This is definitely a step in the right direction, but most dogs could complete these tests by running in a Sanctioned or Licensed Qualifying Stake. If it were known that dogs were running for the W.D.X., I'm sure that judges would schedule the land and water series before the blind retrieves in order to accomodate these dogs. However, I believe that the Chesapeake and Golden Retriever Clubs are the first to initiate tests that require the dog to be steady on line. This is a definite PLUS.

A proud Chessie with the duck he has retrieved.

Another fine retrieve!

23

Champion Black Brant's Decoys Jib and Black Brant's Brandy with the author.

The Chesapeake in Field Trials

When field trials were first held in England, the Flat-Coated and Curly-Coated Retrievers dominated the scene. However, in 1906, The English Kennel Club held its first field trials, and a few Labrador Retrievers were entered to liven things up a bit.

In the United States The Labrador Retriever Club held its first trial during December 1931. It was a specialty trial—for Labradors only. And in 1932 The American Chesapeake Club held its first specialty trial—for Chesapeakes only.

In 1934 the first all-breed Retriever trial was held, and it drew a grand total of fifteen dogs. Contrast that with the entries of the present day and one can see how the sport of field trialing has grown.

The first National Retriever Field Trial was run in 1941 at Long Island, New York. A contemporary account in *The New York Times* lists three Chesapeake Bay Retrievers among the dogs that completed all of the ten tests. They were: Field Trial Champion Sodak's Rip, owned by Earl K. Ward of Fort Smith, Arkansas, and handled by Charles Morgan; Field Trial Champion Shagwong Gypsy, owned and handled by E. Monroe Osborne of East Hampton, Long Island; and Guess of Shagwong, owned by Mr. Osborne and handled by Ed L. Morford.

By 1950 fifty trials were being held each year, and eight years later this number had doubled. As of today there are well over one hundred fifty trials held in this country each year. I would estimate the average entry in the Open All-Age Stake to be nearly sixty dogs per trial.

Quite a few of the trials held in recent years had eighty to ninety entries for the Championship Stakes. Some handlers had sixteen dogs to run at one trial.

Obviously, something must be done, or it will not be possible to conclude the trials in the usual three days.

At the time field trials were first being held in the United States, the Chesapeake was able to compete on a par with any of the other breeds. The Chesapeake thrived during the thirties and forties. Then in the late forties the Labrador began to be more competitive. The two breeds are completely dissimilar in their working habits, the Lab being fast and flashy and the Chesapeake slower, more methodical, and more sure. But judges seemed to lean toward the flashier Lab, and by the mid-fifties, the Chesapeake was on the decline as a field trial dog.

Of course, one analogy shows that the Chesapeake is actually improving in field trial competition. During 1967 Chesapeakes won only nine Open All-Age Stakes during the entire year, while in 1975 the number rose to fourteen. This analogy, however, does not take into account the increase in the number of trials and entries during that space of time.

Presently, Chesapeake field trial dogs are concentrated mainly on the West Coast, where Rex Carr, that great professional trainer, makes a specialty of training the breed for the owners and then turning them back to the owners to be run.

The last of the major kennels of field trial Chesapeakes on the East Coast was South Bay, owned by August and Louise Belmont. The Belmonts had some wonderful field trial dogs during the fifties and early sixties. Then they switched to Labs. They had a very interesting kennel of Chesapeake Bay Retrievers, though, and I intend to tell you more about it later.

Other defectors to the Labrador were Ed and Carol Gesner of Branford, Connecticut. Not many people remember when Ed and Carol had Chessies, but I do. I remember when Ed relied wholeheartedly on the Chesapeake, and I imagine he still does when he goes hunting.

Large kennels on the West Coast include the Mount Joy Kennels of the late Helen Fleischmann and the Baronland Kennels owned by Mrs. Guy Cherry, the former Eloise Heller.

Mount Joy Kennels finished their first field trial champion in 1953. He was Nelgard's King Tut, by Field Trial Champion Chesacroft Baron out of Sunbeam of Cocoa King. Their next was Mount Joy's Mallard, and he, of course, was by Field Trial Champion Nelgard's King Tut. In 1962 Mount Joy's Louistoo finished his field trial championship, and following the progression, he was by Mount Joy's Mallard, who was by then a dual champion.

Incidentally, the AKC titles "Field Trial Champion" and "Field Champion" mean exactly the same thing. So do the titles "Amateur Field Trial Champion" and "Amateur Field Champion." The AKC dropped the word "Trial" from the titles in 1962. In most instances the title that is used is the one that corresponds with the wording in use at the time the title was awarded.

A dual champion, of course, is a dog with both a bench championship and a field championship. Speaking of Chesapeake dual champions, let us see how many there have been.

The first was Dual Champion Sodak's Gypsy Prince, who gained his titles in 1936. He was owned by Chesacroft Kennels. Twenty-three years went by before Mount Joy's Mallard attained the double title. He was also an amateur field champion. As I mentioned previously, he was owned by the Fleischmanns' Mount Joy Kennels.

In 1965, Mrs. Guy Cherry, then Eloise Heller, handled Baron's Tule Tiger to the twin titles. Tiger not only was an amateur field champion as well, but also had the Companion Dog (C.D.) title in obedience.

Also in 1965, Dr. F. A. Dashnaw's Meg's O'Timothey attained the dual titles. Tim also was an amateur field champion and held the coveted Companion Dog Excellent (C.D.X.) title in obedience.

In 1970, Mike Paterno, a comparative newcomer to the Chesapeake ranks, finished Koolwater Colt of Tricrown in the field and on the bench and also as an amateur field champion. I knew Colt well, and he could compete with any breed. His sire was Amateur Field Champion Bomarc of Southbay.

I am sad to report that Mike Paterno passed away suddenly in 1978. He was a tenacious man who trained his own Chesapeakes, and the fancy can ill afford to lose him.

In 1970, Eloise Heller (Mrs. Guy Cherry) finished her second dual champion, Tiger's Cub, who was by Baron's Tule Tiger. According to my records, this was the last Chesapeake to become a dual champion. Because Mrs. Cherry finished two of the six dual champions, it behooves me to include here something about her and her kennel—for she is truly a remarkable woman.

Mrs. Cherry writes, "Chesapeakes have been my hobby since 1939, when I first met one. 'Judge' was a large, husky dog kept down at my husband's duck club, where he was allowed to run loose. There was absolutely no trouble with trespassers when Judge was around. As soon as a car came on the property, he rushed out to meet it, laying back his lips and showing all of his teeth. It was a horrendous smile meant to greet you and say you were welcome, but it seldom was interpreted that way by strangers who didn't know Judge. One look at him and the cars turned around and promptly left the property."

Eloise's first Chessie was one of Judge's pups, and she learned to run in trials with him. He was doing quite well until some little boys who would shoot anything that moved came on the property with a twenty-two caliber rifle.

Eloise's next Chessie was bench Champion Sasnakra Sassy, C.D., who had three sons with field trial championships. And this brings us up to the strange story of Nelgard's Baron.

Eloise purchased Baron at the not-so-tender age of seven. She bought him from Cliff Brignall, who was an excellent trainer but just couldn't communicate with Baron. I believe, though, that Baron did earn some field trial points while Cliff was handling him.

Under Eloise's guidance, Baron finished his field championship within a year. He was her house pet and constant companion and thrived on the affection and attention of this remarkable woman. Baron had 48½

Open All-Age points. He qualified for six Nationals, ran in five, and completed four.

Eloise's next Chessie was one of Baron's sons. He actually had five titles, and his formal description was Dual Champion, Amateur Field Champion, and Canadian Field Champion Baron's Tule Tiger, C.D. Tiger qualified for the astounding total of ten Nationals and was a finalist in four. (A word of explanation to the uninitiated: The Retriever National is run just once each year and includes ten or more grueling and exacting land and water series. Any dog that can complete all of the tests is a truly great Retriever.)

Next came one of Tiger's pups, known formally as Dual Champion and Amateur Field Champion Tiger's Cub, C.D.

It is interesting to note that most of Mrs. Cherry's Chesapeakes have earned the C.D. title in obedience. Usually her dogs earned the obedience title at a young age, and the obedience training was always invaluable for field work.

Getting back to Tiger's Cub—he finished his bench championship in four straight shows, and his obedience title in three straight trials with all scores over 195 out of a possible 200. He won an all-breed Open All-Age Stake when he was just three years old and became a field champion before he was five.

Tiger's Cub ran in six Amateur Nationals from 1969 through 1974. He qualified in 1975 but did not run because Mrs. Cherry was one of the judges. During his career he earned 117 points in licensed field trials, ranking second only to his father, who had a total of 207 points.

Spanning a period of some thirty years, Mrs. Cherry has amassed a record with Chesapeakes that probably will stand for many more years.

Now that I have told you about a major West Coast kennel of Chesapeakes, let's skip back to the East Coast for a look at the South Bay Kennels of August and Louise Belmont. I feel somewhat more relaxed in writing about the Belmonts, for I have known them personally for more than twenty years.

According to Augie, both he and Louise have been involved with dogs all of their lives. Before their marriage, Louise worked with a pack of Beagles and coursed Greyhounds. She also had experience with Terriers and Poodles, and I believe the first dog that Louise finished in obedience was a Poodle.

Augie's father was interested in Pointers, which were bred for use at the family plantation in South Carolina. The family also raised Sealyham Terriers. After Augie and Louise were married, their first dog was a Pointer, and from that dog evolved several litters which were placed in various sections of the country with friends. Unfortunately, the hunting territory in which the

Belmonts lived on Long Island was steadily diminishing in the late forties and the early fifties. During the early fifties, Augie and some of his close friends accumulated some leases for duck shooting in the Manorville area of Long Island near the headwaters of the Peconic River. It soon became evident to them that for this type of hunting they needed a good Retriever. A Chesapeake named Chip of Oldfields arrived shortly thereafter as a gift from some friends.

Chip worked remarkably well in the duck blinds and captured the Belmonts' enthusiasm completely. As a result, they began to look around for a female Chesapeake that eventually could produce some pups by Chip.

In due course, they found the bitch. She was Matilda Manorville. At that time there was an excellent woman field trainer, Dolly Marshall, who lived quite close to the Belmonts. Dolly helped the Belmonts train "Tilly," and persuaded them to let her enter the bitch at a local field trial. The green ribbon that ensued led the Belmonts to the Chesapeake Specialty Trial, and they were "hooked."

Unfortunately, Chip died before it was possible to mate him with Tillie. However, by this time, Tillie had placed in a few Derby Stakes and both of the Belmonts were deeply interested in the breed. They began to ask Chesapeake field trial people about Chesapeake pups.

These people were generous, as most field trial people are, and the Belmonts received gift pups from both Bill Hoard and Ralph Mock. Augie also purchased a pup from Dr. John Lundy for about one hundred dollars. That pup was sired by Dr. Lundy's great Field Champion Atom Bob. His name was Bomarc of South Bay, and he became the Belmonts' one and only amateur field champion of the Chesapeake breed. My wife had the pleasure of handling Bo to his bench championship, which actually made him a dual champion even though he is not listed as such in the Chesapeake year book. Perhaps the year book lists only Chesapeakes that have won Open All-Age field championships.

The Belmonts had greater success with Chessies in the Derby Stakes than in the Championship Stakes. South Bay Nike, a very pretty bitch that they ran in the field and my wife and I showed, had an excellent record in Derby Stakes, but an unfortunate operation ended both her show and field careers and her capacity for breeding. Nike earned a total of eleven Derby points, which placed her high on the Chesapeake Derby list. Matilda Manorville had five Derby points and Bomarc was high on the list with twenty-eight.

Perhaps the Belmonts' best Chesapeake is also the one

that caused them to switch to Labradors. Cherokee South Bay Project, affectionately known as Larry, was that dog. Sired by Bomarc, Larry had an excellent disposition and almost perfect conformation. As a Derby dog in 1964, he not only led all Chessies in total points, but also—with thirty-two points—was fourth leading Derby dog for all breeds. He still ranks as the fourth best Derby dog in Chesapeake history.

But there comes a time when circumstances separate field trial dogs from those that work well in actual hunting. When the Derby is over, the Chesapeake has to learn to work as an Open All-Age dog. I don't say that Larry couldn't do it, but I do say that he wouldn't do it. Louise Belmont had trained him by herself—which is quite a tribute to a gallant gal—but teach him to work as an Open All-Age dog, she could not. Although she had many offers from people who wanted to purchase him, she chose to give him outright to me and my wife. And he gained the distinction of becoming the best gun dog in the country of any breed that I have ever hunted over. For ten years Larry never missed a bird, although to the day he died at the age of fifteen, I could never stop him on a whistle after he had lined out any distance. But after hunting every possibility for some ten minutes, he would look up as if to say, "All right, Boss, where is the bird?"

The Belmonts' Bomarc also compiled quite a field trial record, besides finishing very easily on the bench. By 1980, Bo—with twenty-four points—ranked thirteenth in Amateur points for all Chesapeakes. Bo did not have quite the cheerful disposition that Larry had. Bo was strictly a one-man dog, and woe betide anyone who laid a hand on Augie while Bo was around.

In the show chapter we will come back to the Belmonts and South Bay Kennels, for they made quite a mark in conformation shows as well as in the field.

Even though records and statistics are boring to some people, no breed book would be quite complete without them, so following are the listings of Chesapeake Bay Retriever field champions through December 1980.

Abbreviations that appear in the listings of field champions and amateur field champions include: Can., Canadian; Ch., Champion (bench show); Dual Ch., Dual Champion; F.T.C., Field Trial Champion; F.C., Field Champion; A.F.T.C., Amateur Field Trial Champion; A.F.C., Amateur Field Champion; C.D., Companion Dog; C.D.X., Companion Dog Excellent; and U.D., Utility Dog. The last three are obedience titles and their significance is explained in the chapter on the Chesapeake in obedience competition, while the bench show championships are discussed in the chapters on the Chesapeake in the show ring.

CHESAPEAKE BAY RETRIEVER FIELD CHAMPIONS OF RECORD

Year	Dog	Owner
1935	Skipper Bob (Prince of Montauk—Sou West Sal)	Harry Conklin
1936	Dual Ch. Sodak's Gypsy Prince (Bandy Lindy—Makota's Gypsy Queen)	Chesacroft Kennels
1937	Dilwyne Montauk Pilot (Prince of Montauk—Sou West Sal)	Dilwyne Kennels
1939	Shagwong Gypsy (F.T.C. Skipper Bob—Princess Anne)	E. Monroe Osborne
1941	Sodak's Rip (Dual Ch. Sodak's Gypsy Prince—Chesacroft Darky)	E. K. Ward
1942	Guess of Shagwong (F.T.C. Chesacroft Baron—Shagwong Swamp Fire)	E. Monroe Osborne
1945	Chesacroft Baron (Dual Ch. Sodak's Gypsy Prince—Chesacroft Teal)	
1946	Bayle (Big Chief—Delshore Wilde)	R. N. Crawford
1946	Tiger of Clipper City (F.T.C. Chesacroft Baron—Belle of the Wolf River)	Vance Morris
1952	Deerwood Trigger (Water King Cliff—DelMonte Ginger)	Dr. George Gardner
1952	Montgomery's Sal (Corporal Jan—Klamath Gypsy Nell)	Wm. D Hoard, Jr.
1953	Nelgard's King Tut (F.T.C. Chesacroft Baron—Sunbeam of Cocoa King)	L. P. Montgomery
1954	Raindrop of Deerwood (Johansen's Major—DelMonte Ginger of Deerwood)	Mount Joy Kennels
1959	Can. F.T.C. Nelgard's Baron (Rex of Rapids—F.T.C. Tiger of Clipper City)	P. J. Gagnon
1959	A.F.T.C. Atom Bob (Ch. Nelgard's Riptide—Aleutian Keeko)	Mrs. Walter Heller
1959	Ch. & A.F.T.C. Mount Joy's Mallard (F.T.C. & A.F.T.C. Nelgard's King Tut—Ch. Sasnakra Sassy, C.D.)	Dr. John Lundy E. C. Fleischmann
1960	A.F.T.C. Meg's Pattie O'Rourke (Beewacker's Chester—Meg O'My Heart)	
1960	A.F.T.C. Star King of Mount Joy (F.T.C. & A.F.T.C. Nelgard's King Tut—Ch. Sasnakra Sassy, C.D.)	Dr. F. A.Dashnaw Dr. F. A. Dashnaw
1962	Mount Joy's Louistoo (Dual Ch. & A.F.T.C. Mount Joy's Mallard—Frosty Milady)	E. C. Fleischmann
1963	A.F.T.C. Meg's O'Timothey (Beewacker's Chester—Meg O'My Heart)	Dr. F. A. Dashnaw
1964	Slow Gin (Tealwood's O'Lord Farouk—Lake Lady)	Dr. I. B. Reppert
1965	Ch. Baron's Tule Tiger, C.D. (F.T.C., A.F.T.C. & Can. F.T.C. Nelgard's Baron, C.D.—Joanie Teal)	Mrs. Walter Heller
1966	Chesonoma's Kodiak (A.F.T.C. Chesonoma's Louis—Dinies Miss Priss)	Dr. W. E. Pelzer
1968	A.F.C. Mount Joy's Bit O'Ginger (Dual Ch. & A.F.T.C. Meg's O'Timothey, C.D.X.—Mount Joy's Jug Ears)	Mrs. E. C. Fleischmann
1970	A.F.C. Koolwater Colt of Tritown (A.F.C. Bomarc of South Bay—Welcome of the Willows)	
1970	A.F.C. Tiger's Cub, C.D. (Dual Ch., A.F.C. & Can. F.C. Baron's Tule Tiger, C.D.—Napolitano's Ladybug)	Michael Paterno Eloise Heller
1972	Cub's Kobi King (Dual Ch. & A.F.C. Tiger's Cub, C.D.—Ch. Chesareid April Echo)	
1974	A.F.C. Copper Topper der Wunderbar (Hector—Bonnie La Bonita)	Daniel Hartley
1976	Alamo's Lucius (F.C. & A.F.C. Chesonoma's Kodiak—Dobe's Atom Agnes)	Greg McDaniel
1976	A.F.C. Bay City Jake (Hatchet Man—Ch. Cub's Marin Echo, U.D.)	Ben Robertson
		Peter Van der Mailen & Miles E. Thomas
1978	A.F.C. Aleutian Surf Breaker (The Big Fellow—Chopper's Bobbie)	Dr. Miles Thomas
1979	A.F.C. Chesdel Chippewa Chief (Dual Ch. & A.F.C. Koolwater's Colt of Tricrown—Chesdel Longwood Lassie)	Moncrief A. Spear
1980	Fireweed's Aleutian Widgeon (F.C. & A.F.C. Aleutian Surf Breaker—Ch. Wildwood's Fireweed)	Linda P. Harger
1980	Capital City Jake (F.C. & A.F.C. Bay City Jake—Tawny-Bri)	Jane Kelso

In 1951 The American Kennel Club established a point system under which dogs could earn the title "Amateur Field Trial Champion." Because there is so much repetition in the listings of field champions and amateur field champions, I am listing below only those Chesapeakes that became amateur field champions but did not complete their Open championship. All others are included, of course, in the foregoing list.

CHESAPEAKE BAY RETRIEVER AMATEUR FIELD CHAMPIONS OF RECORD

Year	Dog	Owner
1953	Gypsy (Buddy Brown—Gypsy of Suffolk)	J. V. O'Shea
1954	Odessa Creek Spunky (King Leroy Jan—Montgomery's Sal)	Triever Point Kennels
1955	Chuck's Rip Joy (F.T.C. & A.F.T.C. Nelgard's King Tut—Ch. Sasnakra Sassy, C.D.)	Ralph Mock
1957	Rip (Rip Van Winkle—Raymond's Queenie)	Frank Holliday
1958	Star King of Mount Joy (F.T.C. & A.F.T.C. Nelgard's King Tut—Ch. Sasnakra Sassy, C.D.	Harold Johnson
1959	Chesonoma's Louis (Dual Ch. & A.F.T.C. Mount Joy's Mallard—Ch. Frosty Milady)	Winston Moore
1963	Ch. Bomarc of South Bay, C.D. (F.T.C. & A.F.T.C. Atom Bob—Aleutian Duchess)	August Belmont
1975	Can. F.C. & Can. A.F.C. Nanuck of Cheslang (The Big Fellow—Atomalina Myrtle)	Hans Kuck

A list of Chesapeakes with five or more Derby points is of interest, regardless of what these dogs did after Derby competition. If you compare this list with the lists of field champions and amateur field champions, you will see how few Chesapeakes went on to earn those titles.

All of the Derby points were garnered in Licensed Trials and the system for scoring is the same as the systems currently used for scoring championship points: five points for first place, three for second, one for third, and one-half for fourth.

In making comparisons, remember that a dog amassing fifty or so points may have participated in almost a hundred trials to do so, while a dog with fifteen points may have run and won only three Derby Stakes. Also, dogs amassing points in the forties and fifties had many less trials to enter than dogs amassing points in the late sixties and early seventies. Be that as it may, following is the list of dogs and owners.

Hunter with Chesapeake and birds retrieved.

CHESAPEAKES WITH FIVE OR MORE DERBY POINTS

Dog	Owner	Points	Dog	Owner	Points
Meg's Pattie O'Rourke	Dr. F. A. Dashuaw	90	Mister Chips	Robert Volger	8
Baron's Tule Tiger	Eloise Heller	55	Tawney's Little Joey	Paul DeLong	8
Tiger's Cub	Eloise Heller	37	Aleutian Surfbreaker	J. McRoberts & Dr. M. Thomas	7
Cherokee South Bay Project	August Belmont	32	Chesareid April Echo	Eloise Heller	7
Chesdel Chippewa Chief	M. A. Spear	31	Cub's Wild Turkey	Eloise Heller	7
Kilmore's Thundering Turk	John Smith III	30	Mount Joy's Mighty Ike	Mrs. E. C. Fleischmann	7
Bomarc of South Bay	August Belmont	28	Prune Face	Eloise Heller	7
Meg's Tami O'Hara	Dr. Miles Thomas	24	Shamrock Cap	R. L. Ireland	7
Capitol City Jake	Eloise Cherry	23	Beewacker's Jeff	Morris Aboauf	6
Mount Joy's Bit O'Ginger	Barbara Ornbaun	21	Chesonoma's Kodiak	Dr. W. E. Peltzer	6
Mount Joy's Mallard	E. C. Fleischmann	18	King Tut's Sassy Cokey	M. Hockaday	6
Slow Gin	Dr. L. B. Reppert	18	Welcome of the Willows	Margaret Long	6
Mount Joy's E. C. Bay	F. & J. Nicholes	17	Alpine Bay Lady	J. DeMaster	5
Baron's Bangaway	Eloise Heller	16	Buddy Cafe AuLait	A. Johnson	5
Chesdel Potlatch Charley	M. A. Spear	16	Charon's Cerberus	Dr. L. T. Brice	5
Hatchet Man	C. E. Cannedy	16	Chesonoma's Louis	E. C. Fleischmann	5
Beewacker's Chester	E. J. Rowe	15	Chessie Cocoa Nut	William Brocket	5
The Big Fellow	Dr. John Lundy	14	Wingfoot Spike	Ray Brown	5
Alpine Big Butch	Marie Woodall	13	Whitewater Ike	Carl Barfuss	5
Mount Joy's Jug Ears	E. C. Fleischmann	13	Tommy Trojan	Dr. John Lundy	5
Platte River Jane	Eloise Heller	12	Toba Buster of Peake	Cyril Hicks	5
Blue Valley Jimbo	Robert Ray, Jr.	11	Rooks' Blasting Cap	Jim Ray	5
Meg's O'Malley II	C. Sambrailo, Jr.	11	Raincoat Charlie Brown	Burt Ebaugh	5
Red Trail of Echo Lake	C. D. Rankin, Jr.	11	Now Then of Deerwood	P. J. Gagnon	5
South Bay Nike	August Belmont	11	Matilda Manorville	August Belmont	5
Alamo's Lucias	Ben Robertson	10	Little Drake	Jake Nance	5
Baronland's Ginger	Rudy Trevino	10	Kodi's Boomerang	Dr. W. E. Peltzer	5
Mount Joy's Dilwyne Jez O'Meg	J. Mitchell & R. Carpenter	10	Kilmore's Lightship	John Smith III	5
Cocoa of Rocky River	Don Gearhart	9	Jake's Elizah	Pete Van Der Meulen	5
Missy's South Bay Pasquale	August Belmont	9	J. F. Hinks' Gus of Monte Vista	Marilyn Hinks	5
Mount Joy's Louistoo	E. C. Fleischmann	9	Gypsy Rover	John Folsom	5
Mount Joy's Rowdy	August Belmont	9	Dobe's Atom Agnes	Dr. W. E. Peltzer	5
Stratte's Norske	Dr. Paul Stratte	9	Cub's Thunder Bumper	Margaret Woolsey	5
Alpine Billie's Chips	J. D. Conley	8	Copper Topper der Wunderbar	Greg McDaniel	5
Atom Bob	Dr. John Lundy	8	Cocoa Prince of Kent	Murray Sim	5
Chesareid Donachie Topper	William DuBuse	8			

Ed Fleischmann and Field Champion Bayberry Pete. Ed was a moving force in Chesapeakes, and his loss is sorely felt.

30

Mount Joy Kennels

An account of Chesapeakes in field trials would not be complete without the story of the late Ed and Helen Fleischmann and their Mount Joy Kennels, one of the oldest Chesapeake kennels in the United States.

Helen sent me a running account of their dogs, and I include it here much as she wrote it.

"My late husband's main interests in life were hunting and fishing, and he rarely let business interfere with those pursuits. Sometime in the early 1930s, Melville Baruh (Melando Kennels) gave Ed a Chesapeake puppy from Louis Traung's Grizzly Island Kennels, and so started a lifelong love affair with the Chesapeake breed.

"About the time Ed retired from business in the mid-forties, field trial clubs were starting on the West Coast and Ed became interested in training his dogs for field trials as well as for hunting. Very few people knew anything about field trials and assumed that a good hunting dog would make a good field trial dog. Of course things were much simpler then, and, I might add, much more fun.

"Ed took a trip to the East Coast and also to the Midwest and met many of the old-time Chesapeake breeders—Anthony Bliss, Monroe Osborne, Ferdinand Bunte, Arthur Stertz, Phil Gagnon, Bob Brown, Bill Hoard, John Lundy, and many others. He also bought Bayberry Pete from Dr. Parrot for running trials and use as a stud dog.

"Pete was a really great marking dog, especially on water, but he was never too easy to handle, for he was convinced he knew where everything was—and he was generally right. He was also a very beautiful animal. The pups he sired were generally pretty mediocre, but one nice thing was that they usually inherited Pete's marking ability.

"At that time it was very difficult for a Chesapeake to win because there were so few of them, but Pete was second highest point dog in the country with seconds, thirds, and fourths for one year.

"He finished his life as Ed's hunting dog, and since few of the members of his hunting club had dogs, he retrieved the hard ones for all twenty-five members.

"We bred and bought many dogs, but through lack of knowledge of training, we won in only a few trials. In late 1951, Bob Brown, then owner of Mount Joy Kennels, gave us a pup that we named Mount Joy's Mallard. At that time we were using the kennel name of Chesonoma, for we live in Sonoma County in California.

"One of the first pups Mallard sired was the first pup I trained myself, Chesonoma's Louis. Louis got second in an Amateur Stake when he was two and a half years old. We sold him to Winston Moore, who was more interested in hunting than in field trials. He kept a log on how many ducks Louis retrieved out of Snake River. I can't remember what year it was that Winston wrote me that Louis had that day retrieved his duck number 3,000. (That, dear readers, is a lot of ducks.)

"We had become good friends with Bob and Jesse Brown. Jesse Brown died and a few years later Bob also passed away. Since we owned Mount Joy's Mallard and were using him as our principal stud, we acquired the Mount Joy name.

"Mallard became the first dual and amateur field trial champion in the Chesapeake breed. Field Trial Champion and Amateur Field Champion Louistoo, sired by Mallard, became the fifth in a line of field champion Chesapeakes.

"Louistoo was also the only Chesapeake to win two double-headers in all-breed competition and remains the only two-time Chesapeake winner until this date. ("Double-header," as used here, means that the dog won the Open All-Age Stake and the Amateur All-Age Stake at the same trial.)

"In our breeding program we tried to avoid 'kennel blindness' and bred to every good dog in the country. Field Trial Champion and Amateur Field Trial Champion Atom Bob, owned by Dr. John C. Lundy, was the grandson of Bayberry Pete. We had a bitch from Deerwood Kennels owned by Phil Gagnon. Gagnon, of course, owned Field Trial Champion Raindrop of Deerwood. We had bitches from Ferd Bunte's Cocoa Kennels, and Mallard's daughter Trofast of Green Valley was the granddam of Dual Champion and Amateur Field Champion Baronlands Tiger, owned by Eloise Heller Cherry.

"Mount Joy's Bit O'Ginger was sired by Dual Champion and Amateur Field Trial Champion Meg's O'Timothy, C.D.X., whose grandsire was Meland Happy Jack, my husband's hunting dog.

"Mallard was an excellent marking dog and had a wonderful disposition. Most of his faults were man-made. His disposition seems to be carried on in almost all of his progeny.

"Louistoo was a truly fantastic marker on water and a great line-running dog. There are many dogs that could mark with him on land, but I don't believe any dog could mark with him consistently on water. Bit O'Ginger was not quite as good a marker as Louis, but had much more style and speed.

"My present dog, Mount Joy's Mighty Ike, is really a good all-around dog and I feel that had I been able to run him myself, he would have a much better record. He is so attached to me that he never really does his best for anyone else. If he knows that I am around, he really

Above, Field Champion and Amateur Field Champion Mount Joy's Bit O'Ginger, owned by Helen Fleischmann. Ginger was the only Chesapeake qualified for the National Open Stake held in November 1969 at Dover, Delaware, and ran very well in that stake.

Below, Champion Mount Joy's Louistoo at the 1962 National Retriever Field Trial. Louistoo was never handled by anyone but Helen Fleischmann.

'loses his marbles' until he finds me, which doesn't do his marking or behavior any good.

"My husband and I were the first people to make three field champions in the Chesapeake breed, and I had great hopes for making the fourth with the Mount Joy name, but I don't think I will make it. (A Chesapeake very rarely runs as well for anyone else as he does for his owner. A Chesapeake has a definite tendency to be a one-person dog and rarely relaxes completely unless that person is by his side.)

"At present, it is pretty much the rule that almost all of the Chesapeakes at field trials and a great many at both the shows and obedience trials are from Dr. John Lundy's Aleutian Kennel, Eloise Cherry's Baronland, or my Mount Joy, or a combination of the three. (This is just about completely true in the western half of the country, but there are some eastern show dogs and obedience dogs of different breeding. These three kennels completely dominate the field trial scene, though.)

"Louistoo was always sterile, to my very great disappointment, so to carry on the Mallard line, I bred to his full brother, Mount Joy's Mighty, owned by Winston Moore, to produce my present dog, Mount Joy's Mighty Ike.

"When Ginger was in Derby, I naturally wanted her to win the Chesapeake Specialty Derby. She was due in season just at that time, so I had her given a drug to keep her from coming in season. The drug worked and she did win, but it was the most expensive win I ever made. She did eventually come in season again, but almost died. This also happened the next time she came in, which was within the space of a year. Finally the vet thought she could be bred, and I bred her to a very indifferent dog, for he was the only one that I had around at the time. She suffered so that I gave all the pups away as soon as possible and hoped I would never hear of them again—which I haven't. She died of cancer of the liver at seven years of age. She had worked the day before and the vet could not believe she had walked into the hospital where she died that afternoon. She was truly one of the greatest and toughest bitches that I have ever known."

It is essential to note that none of the drugs currently on the market to alter seasons is safe, and some are actually lethal.

The dog Mrs Fleischmann especially wanted Ginger to defeat was Cherokee's South Bay Project (Larry), owned at that time by Louise Belmont. Larry went on to win the Derby title that year, and, as mentioned before, later was the author's hunting dog.

Ed Fleischmann died in 1969 and Helen died in July 1978. They were grand people. Although I did not know them personally, I had volumes of correspondence with Helen during the last year of her life. Included in the letters she wrote me were the history of Mount Joy Kennels, which you have just read, and many "salty" comments on personalities in the Chesapeake world— comments which I treasure. I felt that I knew Helen well, even though I was never privileged to meet her. She not only will be sorely missed by the Chesapeake fancy but also will never be replaced.

Mount Joy's Mighty Ike making a successful retrieve. Handler, Chuck Crook.

Left and right: The author demonstrates the proper techniques for teaching the "Stay" command.

Left: A Mount Joy pup dreaming dreams of grandeur.

Right: A little puppy demonstrates the proper way to carry a big bumper.

Left and right: Champion Black Brant's Decoys Jib waits for her turn to retrieve. Handler, Ruth Beaman.

34

Early Training for Your Chesapeake Pup

With a title such as the above, I think I had better go with you when you buy your Chesapeake pup and see that you get one that is worth training.

The first question that comes to mind is "Dog or bitch?" The obvious drawback to the female, is, of course, that she comes in season approximately once every six months and cannot be run in trials at that time and usually cannot be used for hunting during that period, either. On the plus side are the facts that you can breed her and that a female is usually more tractable in training than a male is.

Say, for our purposes, that we have settled on a male. What should we look for? First, don't feel sorry for the cute little pup huddling in the corner. Have your eye out for a big, aggressive pup that pushes everything out of his way to get to you. Now, look for a second pup with similar traits and ask to take these first two choices out of the kennel and make sure that they are just as aggressive away from their brothers and sisters. Then make your choice.

Of course we have previously checked the pedigree and found a good number of field champions, or at least several with Working Certificates (W.C.'s) close up.

The price of the pup will depend on how good the pedigree is. And, believe me, a good pup is worth a good price. Remember that it costs just as much to feed a poor specimen as a good one, and the cost of feed and care will far exceed the purchase price.

Now a word about the breed and why a Chesapeake is trained differently from the other Retrievers. Stating it baldly, the Chesapeake definitely has a mind of his own and will try to get away with anything he can unless you are very strict.

A good example is a Chesapeake my wife and I own. He was introduced to the house at the tender age of six weeks. The first time my wife tried to remove his food dish, he growled and snapped at her. Naturally he received a slap on the muzzle, but he continued to keep his tail wagging. He had just learned that growling and snapping constituted a "no-no." He never tried guarding his food again. I cite this example because many neophytes in Chessies—and probably neophytes in all breeds—will think that guarding the food is cute. Permitting it might be a disastrous mistake. Permitting it certainly will make your training much more difficult. Also watch for excessive guarding of his toys or even his bed. You should be able to handle any of your pup's

belongings without the slightest objection from him.

You must keep your Chesapeake under control at all times. This is true of any breed, but it is a "must" with the Chesapeake.

Another thing that applies to all breeds but is important enough to deserve mention here, is to take care to maintain your pup's health. In selecting your pup, you would have made sure that he appeared to be in good health and the breeder would have given you a record of the types of "puppy shots" he had received and the dates he got them. Take your pup to your veterinarian as soon as possible, and take the health record with you. NEVER LEAVE YOUR PUP WITH YOUR VETERINARIAN FOR TREATMENT UNLESS THAT IS ABSOLUTELY NECESSARY. Have your pup's stool checked for worms and if he needs worming, ask your veterinarian for the worm medicine. Worm him yourself. And be sure to follow your veterinarian's advice on scheduling inoculations to be given later.

Now that the veterinary care is out of the way, let us assume that you have a healthy, happy pup and are ready to begin his early training.

Make a bed for the pup in the kitchen or wherever you want him to sleep. Give him his food in the same area, close to his bed. He must learn that this is where he is to eat and sleep.

"Kennel" is a command that should be taught as soon as your Chessie comes into his new home. This command may be used not only to instruct the dog to enter his bed, crate, or kennel, but also to enter the car, a particular room, or anywhere else you want him to go. If you repeat the command "Kennel" and show the puppy exactly where you want him to go—lifting him and placing him in his bed or crate, if necessary—he will learn this command easily and at an early age. And, believe me, you will find that this is one of the most useful commands your Chessie knows.

Take your pup outdoors early and often. He'll make mistakes, but probably not many. In less than a week you will find that your pup goes to the door or gives you some kind of signal when he wants to go out. Just watch him carefully in the early stages and you won't have much trouble with housebreaking. The Chesapeake is a very clean breed.

Most Chesapeake pups are just about impervious to ill effects from bad weather. Following a March storm in which more than two feet of snow was dumped on us, our pup's greatest pleasure was to go outside, do what he had to do, and then lie down in the deepest snowdrift he could find. Chesapeakes adapt just as readily to warm weather and especially enjoy opportunities to work at water retrieving once temperatures moderate.

I assume you are interested in using your Chesapeake

in the field, so now comes the question, "When can we start field training?" Well, you can start right now if you just remember two things: first, every aspect of field training must be fun to your pup; second, your pup's attention span is quite short at this age, so don't worry if he forgets from day to day. As he gets older he will remember and the early training will pay off.

First, let's train your pup to come when called. This is simple. Use his food for a reward. When his food is ready, give the command "Come" along with his name. He'll come—don't worry.

Now you will need to purchase a plastic whistle with a lanyard so that you can wear it around your neck. After a few days, besides calling your pup vocally, start using one long and two short blasts of your whistle. In a short time you will find that besides dispensing with the voice command you will be over at least the first hurdle of teaching field commands. Just remember one thing: always reward your Chesapeake when he comes to the whistle—at least at this tender age of six to twelve weeks.

The command "Sit," which comes next, is easy to teach. When your pup comes to you for his food, say "Sit," and ease him into the sit position at your left side. At first, keep him there only a moment or two and then release him by saying "O.K." In a few days he will sit automatically and remain sitting until you release him. Then you can start substituting one short whistle blast for the vocal command to sit. This is step number two toward future valuable field training.

At this point, you may as well teach your pup the command "Down." Although it is not used in field trials, it will prove invaluable later on, when you are teaching your Chessie hunting and gun dog work.

First put your pup in the sit position and then give him the command "Down," at the same time pressing gently on his shoulders until he is down. If this proves difficult, attach a leash to your dog's choke chain and stand in front of him, holding the leash. Give him the command "Down," and if he doesn't obey, apply pressure with your foot on the leash, making it tighten and literally forcing your dog to the down position. Repeat this as often as necessary until he will obey the command itself. There is no whistle command for down.

Now let's suppose that your pup is eight weeks of age and you are anxious to try some retrieving with him. First, you should purchase a small boat bumper that your pup can handle easily. For the novice, various size boat bumpers may be purchased at most marine stores. Many companies specializing in Retriever supplies also carry them. I prefer the canvas bumpers to the plastic ones. Although the canvas bumpers don't last as long, there is less tendency for the dog to become "hard mouthed." ("Hard mouthed" is the term used to describe a dog that bites or marks with his teeth the game he retrieves, or a dog that will not release the bird to the handler.)

For this early training, take your pup out on a level field. First, give him the one short whistle blast to command him to sit at your left, for we might as well start him correctly. Now throw the boat bumper about twenty feet in front of him so that he can see it easily. At almost the same time, give him the command "Back" (the verbal command usually used to direct a dog to retrieve), and simultaneously move your left arm forward—which is the visual signal for him to retrieve. If your pup is confused, you may have to give him the command "Back" again, but usually a pup will be there before the bumper hits the ground. As soon as your pup picks up the bumper, give the command "Come." If that command is well ingrained, your pup will automatically return to you with the bumper, but don't be upset if he doesn't. If he starts to run away with the bumper, turn and run away from him, calling at the same time for him to come. Nine times out of ten he will reverse his direction and come right to you. After all, the fun is in having you chase him, and if you don't, he will chase you.

If you have a great deal of trouble getting the pup to deliver the bumper to you, don't force the issue. Wait until your pup is a little older and then use one of the following methods.

The first method is simple. Send your pup on a short retrieve. When he has picked up the bumper and has started in, tell him to come and at the same time move away from him, making him follow you. He very likely will continue to hold the bumper. Now turn suddenly and take the bumper from him. Praise him immediately and lavishly, and repeat the exercise. Before long your pup will automatically bring the bumper to hand.

If you are having trouble at a little later age, here is a procedure that usually is successful. If your dog drops the bumper at your feet or somewhere near you, give him the command to sit and stay. Now pick up the bumper, place it between his jaws, and say "Hold it." You may have to do this several times for him to grasp your meaning. You also might have to press his lower and upper jaws together—but do it gently! After he sits and holds the bumper, walk five or ten feet away from him, then turn to face him and tell him to come. When he comes, either tell him to heel, still holding the bumper, or just take the bumper from him.

You might think that we are starting the Chesapeake puppy too young on too much, but that is not so. Your Chesapeake pup is tough. He is much tougher than a pup of the other Retriever breeds. That is why it is important that you start his training while he is young. I have already warned you about allowing him to guard

In these four photos, Ruth Beaman is seen teaching her Chesapeake, Spinner, that picking up decoys is a "no-no."

Above: A Chessie pup demonstrates the incorrect way to carry a bumper.

Below: Another demonstration of the right way to carry a bumper.

Above: He demonstrates the correct way to carry a bumper.

Below: This pup, too, shows the wrong way to carry a bumper.

Below: This pup apparently wonders whether he is expected to show or to retrieve.

The Chessie is trained to sit immediately when he hears one short blast of the whistle.

38

objects, but it is important that you gain your pup's respect. He must grow up to be a good field dog and a good pet, but with the ability to use his own mind, too.

Let's get back to retrieving. If your pup won't retrieve without training, forget about using him for field work. Some breeds of Sporting Dogs have to be "force broken" to retrieve, but don't even think of that with a Chesapeake. You have to teach your pup a lot, but running out to retrieve a boat bumper or shot bird should be as natural to him as eating and sleeping.

You might think that all Chesapeakes retrieve naturally and love the water. This is not true. I particularly remember two Chesapeakes which were sent to my wife and me for field training many years ago. Both were completely show bred, except that both were sired by a field champion. One of them would do simple retrieves, but as soon as the bumper or bird was thrown more than twenty feet out into the water, he would refuse to retrieve it. The other dog was worse. He would retrieve, but when he delivered, he would immediately attack his handler, going for the throat—no less. We cured him of that, but he also lost interest in retrieving.

You see, there are many types of Chesapeakes, and most of them can retrieve, but again I warn you, before you buy a pup, make sure there are plenty of known field dogs close up in the pup's pedigree.

The most formative stage of a puppy's development is between six and twelve weeks of age. Recently this has been proven by various scientific laboratories, although I have known it for more than twenty years.

There are a few "do's and don'ts" you must remember if you are training your youngster during the early spring. It is all right for your pup to swim voluntarily, but it is wrong for you to send him into the water when it is cold. If he enters the water on his own, praise him, but don't throw his bumper in, making him retrieve it. The shock of the near-freezing temperature could give your pup a mental block about the water. I will admit that this happens rarely with Chesapeakes, but you should be aware that it can occur. Mud puddles and shallow running water are all right, but in the early spring, be careful about sending your pup into water that is deep enough so that he will have to swim.

After your Chessie pup is retrieving well on open ground, he is ready to work in an area with some light cover: ditches, low stone walls, and similar obstacles. This should be at the age of about twelve weeks.

Familiarization is the most important first step in introducing your pup to this type of training. In other words, before attempting any retrieving, make sure you walk your pup in, over, and around all of the obstacles. He should be thoroughly familiar with the entire area before you throw anything for him. If he isn't, he might hurt himself or become discouraged easily.

My wife has a good method for training a pup to jump ditches. She takes the pup to the ditch and jumps over it herself, encouraging the pup to do the same. The first few times he tries it, he will not know how to jump and will go straight up. Naturally he will fall into the ditch. Eventually, though, he will learn and will jump the ditch right along with her. Then he is ready to retrieve over the ditch—but not before.

At this point in his training, always use just one bumper, never more. Allow the pup to concentrate completely on this one object. When he jumps the ditch, and picks up the bumper and returns to you, be lavish in your praise even though you may feel foolish. Lavish praise will pay off. Remember you are training an eight-week-old pup, not an eight-month-old one.

This Chessie swims directly toward the bumper he has been sent to retrieve.

Now he proudly returns with the bumper held securely between his jaws.

The same principle will apply with low cover and stone walls. Always walk the pup through the cover and over the walls, allowing him to see exactly what he is getting into. Then, and only then, start with the retrieving.

As soon as possible in this phase of training, have someone go along and throw the bumper for you. If you throw the bumper (or bird) for too long, your dog will think he should bring the bumper or bird back to whoever threw it, and this can prove troublesome later on in Derby Stakes or in any type of field trials.

When my wife and I are training a Chesapeake pup, I throw the bumper while my wife handles the pup, and then she throws the bumper while I handle him. That way, the pup soon learns to bring the "bird" to whoever is handling him. Believe me, this is important. You might not think so as you read this, but as soon as you start training your first Chesapeake, you'll see what I mean. And in this early training, always remember that you are training a pup that is between the ages of six and twelve weeks, not six and twelve months. There is a vast difference between the two.

Before ending this chapter on early training, I am going to show you just how to test your young Chesapeake on retrieving ability. For testing, you will need the following equipment: a plastic whistle with lanyard, to hang around your neck; three or four 3" x 12" canvas boat bumpers with ropes attached; if possible, a "starter" pistol for use in shooting blank cartridges; and, above all, a lot of patience.

If you adhere to the basic principles shown in the sketch, you very likely will think of other tests by which you can judge your pup's skill in retrieving.

First, remove the cord from the bumper. This is very important. The cord is attached to the bumper for use in throwing the bumper long distances, but a young pup will tend to play with the cord rather than grab the bumper. Hence, no cord, no temptation to play. The distance shown in the sketch is self-explanatory, and you can vary it as your pup improves in retrieving ability. When you try this test for the first time, the ground cover should not be heavy. It should, however, suffice to hide the bumper, for one of the things you are instilling in your pup is the practice of using his nose as well as his eyes. If the bumper is in plain sight, he tends to forget to use his nose.

The last factor shown on the land sketch is the wind direction. Preferably, the wind should be coming straight into the pup's nose—which also will encourage him to use his nose to good advantage.

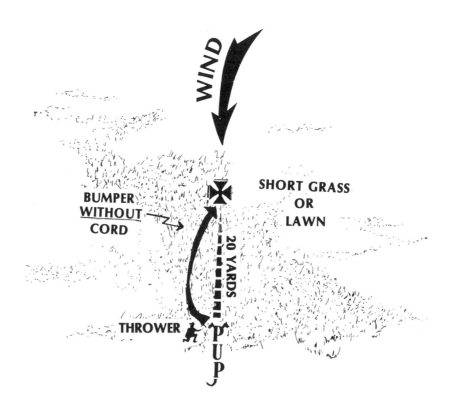

Starting Pup—Land

40

Now we go on to the second sketch, which shows a test for water retrieving. If possible, find an area similar to the one shown in the sketch, with level ground or a beach, then shallow running water, and then warm open water. It is essential that the water be warm, for when a young Chesapeake pup is introduced to water, he is eager and will plunge right in. As noted earlier, if the water is icy—as it is in many areas of the United States in the winter and on into March, April, or even May—the pup will receive an unpleasant shock and might not be quite so eager to enter the water the next time. Whenever possible, don't introduce your pup to water unless it is warm—say from June through September.

Again, make sure to remove the cord from the bumper. For retrieving from water, this is even more important than for retrieving on land, for in the water a pup will be likely to grab the cord and "tow" the bumper in, rather than to grasp the bumper firmly in his mouth as he should. Again, the wind should be coming straight into the pup's nose to help him "mark" the place where the bumper landed. (That is, note and remember where it landed.)

Be sure to remember another important point: most pups like the water retrieving better than the land retrieving and tend to play with the bumper before bringing it to the handler. This is where your whistle comes into use. As soon as your Chesapeake grasps the bumper, blow one long and two short blasts on the whistle, telling him to come. If this doesn't work, use

the voice command to come. No matter what happens, though, no punishment should be administered at this stage of his training even if you have to take a swim.

The following are the two most important principles in the early training of a Chesapeake pup that is between the ages of six and twelve weeks:

First is training the pup to come immediately to the whistle command. This instills obedience in your pup and is the basis for all other commands. It also keeps your pup from investigating interesting scents along the way, and helps to keep him from "tasting" the "bird" once he has located it and picks it up.

Second is training him to sit immediately when he hears the one short blast of the whistle. Besides steadying your pup somewhat, this makes the delivery of the bird much easier. Delivery of the bird can be a problem with Chesapeakes, so this early training can be invaluable. IMMEDIATE RESPONSE TO THE WHISTLE COMMAND TO SIT ALSO CAN BE IMPORTANT LATER ON IN TEACHING ADVANCED HANDLING.

In general, this chapter was intended to help you in getting to know your pup and to help him in getting to know you. This not only makes further training easier, but also will be invaluable in advanced training.

In later chapters, I will deal with intermediate and advanced training, with emphasis on facets of training that are peculiar to the Chesapeake.

If you have performed your early lessons well, you will look forward to the later chapters.

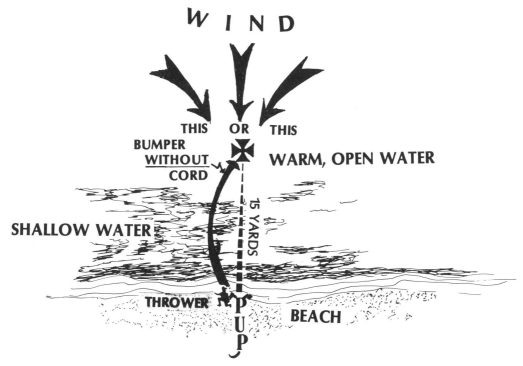

Starting Pup—Water

41

Left: Field Champion and Amateur Field Champion Mount Joy's Bit O'Ginger, owned by Helen Fleischmann. Photo by Bennett Associates.

Right: A Chessie in action, photographed by *The New York Times.*

Left: Champion Count Chocula, C.D., owned by Elizabeth Gough and being handled here by a friend who does not wish to be identified. Photo by A. Gough.

42

Intermediate Field Training for Your Chesapeake Pup

By intermediate training, I mean training for competition through Derby Stakes, with just a touch of handling thrown in.

A dog is eligible for Derby Stakes until he reaches two years of age. At that time he graduates to Qualifying Stakes, and a bit later on, if he proves to be good enough, to Open All-Age and Amateur All-Age competition. At least this is the theory.

The first thing you must do in starting your Chesapeake on his Derby days is to teach him to count. Yes, you heard me, to count! Derby tests usually consist of two birds on land, water, or both, being shot while your dog stands quietly by your side. This is when he must count. He must "mark" both birds. That is, he must note and remember the location where each bird lands after it is thrown and shot. In Derby Stakes you then send your dog after the last bird first—after the judge has called your number, of course.

To start training your dog on retrieving two birds, you will need assistants—either two bird throwers with shotguns and popper shells, or two bird throwers and two "Guns" to do the shooting. Loud yells will suffice some of the time if you are using dead birds, but use shotguns and shells as much as possible.

In the beginning, this training should take place in an open field so that both of the birds will be in plain sight when they are thrown and your dog can mark both of them.

Position your throwers far apart from one another, one to your extreme left and the other to your extreme right. The reason for this is to prevent your dog from running out, picking up one bird, and then running over and trying to pick up the second one and bring them both in at once. No matter how honorable his intentions are, this is a definite "no-no" in field trials. This also is not a good situation when actually hunting, for the dog usually will become totally confused and bring in nothing.

As soon as your young Chesapeake has picked up the first bird, blow the long and two short blasts on your whistle, and keep it up. If he shows signs of switching birds (going to the other bird), start calling him. Under no circumstances let him drop the bird he was sent to

retrieve and pick up the other one. This is the main reason that the birds should be far apart, and that you should be in a position to block the dog if he does not perform as he should.

The first few days or even the first few times you attempt the double retrieves will determine whether or not you will have trouble with your dog "switching." If both dead and live birds are used at this point, make sure that the second bird shot is a flyer (that is, a live bird). Then your young Chessie will be more likely to bring it in to you before going for the other one. The foregoing takes it for granted that your dog can count to two (that is, remember two birds). But what if he can't? If, after you have drilled him for several months, he still gives you a blank stare when you send him for the second bird, forget about training him for field trials.

Fortunately, most Chesapeakes are extremely good markers and can count up to two and usually to three with no trouble.

Now, let's assume that your young dog is doing fairly lengthy double retrieves on open ground. Then we come to the next step—retrieving from cover.

At first, don't work in an area where the cover is heavy, but make sure of two things: that your dog CANNOT see the birds after they fall, and that he CAN see the Guns and bird throwers.

The reason for the latter will be readily understood. If your dog is a good marker, he will go immediately to the bird. If, however, he has mismarked, he probably will run to the Guns, go ten paces in the direction the bird was thrown, and bend down and pick it up. This is not good, but it's much better than for him not to find the bird at all.

Remember too that you must never let your Guns or throwers help your dog if he has mismarked. If you permit them to help him, he soon will learn to rely on their help instead of hunting the bird out himself. Go out there yourself and help him if need be. If your dog becomes discouraged and starts to come in to you, move fast and go out to him with a sharp NO!

Let us assume that your Chesapeake pup is now nine months of age and that he makes respectable double retrieves in cover on land and single retrieves in the water. Now comes the big moment: double retrieves in the water—and, believe me, this is a phase of training that is beset with difficulties. The main one, of course, is that when your dog is in the water, you can't get to him to correct him. In the summer, with some recalcitrant pupils, I used to wear bathing trunks while training so that I could go into the water when necessary, but the black flies bit too hard to continue to do so.

Again, when starting double retrieves in water, never throw the two birds in close proximity. Have as much space between them as possible. You might say that much water is not available. I reply, hunt for it. A small pond where your Chesapeake will learn every possible mistake is worse than no water at all.

Naturally, we cannot go into all of the faults your pup may acquire while learning to retrieve in water, but let's take up a few of them.

First and foremost is "bank running." When the second bird is thrown, your dog, instead of entering the water straight on, may run to the Guns and then enter the water. This is not because he wants to disobey you, but because he wants to retrieve the birds as quickly as possible.

I have never been able to understand why field trial judges penalize so harshly for bank running if the dog enters the water smartly and comes back with the bird promptly. In hunting, unless one is hunting in a populated area, bank running is an asset rather than a liability, especially for retrieving cripples. However, in field trials bank running is a "no-no," so try your best to prevent it.

A second problem is that trick of switching birds, the same as on land. The trouble in water retrieving is that it is much harder for you to get to your dog. Therefore, make doubly sure that the two birds are thrown far apart. If possible, have them thrown into two bodies of water. Often there are man-made lakes available with a dike between. If you work from the dike, even though you have to turn your dog to watch each bird fall, you will find that it is well worth the effort in the long run. As soon as your Chesapeake learns that he is to bring you the bird that was shot second before retrieving the one that was shot first, your problem will be solved. Here is an example of how well it will be solved. Some time ago I was hunting with my combination field trial and hunting Chesapeake on a large lake with heavy cover. In a once-in-a-lifetime effort, I shot two Canada geese. The first was a clean kill, the second a wing tip with the bird gliding down several hundred yards away. My big dog took off and passed the dead goose as if it were not there. About half an hour later, he returned by the same route with a large, very much alive goose in his mouth, again not deigning to look at the dead bird. Only after delivering his burden very carefully, did he turn, swim out leisurely, and retrieve the dead bird. This is a type of sagacity that is evidenced much more often in the Chesapeake than in any other Retriever breed.

Now, let us assume that your dog is doing simple double retrieves in open water with reasonable accuracy. It is time to switch to cover, and the main thing to remember is to do it gradually.

Begin by giving your dog one bird in cover and the second in the open. Again, this will be a test of his memory and whether he can count to two. However, if

he was capable of counting to two on land, you can be sure that he will be able to do the same in water, so don't worry about it. Start by having the first bird fall into cover with the second in plain sight. After your dog has mastered this situation, then give him two birds in cover, and as he becomes more proficient, increase the difficulties of the two retrieves.

At this stage, if your dog has mastered double retrieves both on land and in water and with difficult cover, and is completely steady to shot, then both of you are ready for Derby Stakes.

Before going any further, let me give you a suggestion. If you can find a field trial club that holds training sessions, or even a small group of people with Retrievers who want to train their dogs, you will do well to work with them. However, don't allow them to tell you what to do. Just cooperate by throwing birds for them and then when it is your turn, set up your own tests and let them do the throwing and shooting. Too many dogs have been ruined by naive amateurs offering well-meant but wrong advice. Trust only good professional trainers or good training books.

There is a field trial club in our area, and my wife and I work our Chesapeake with them. But club members act merely as Guns and throwers, and, naturally, we reciprocate. Any well-meant advice goes in one ear and out the other. Remember this. It is important.

Well, here we are with your dog at the age of about ten months, and you really believe that he just might be ready for the Derby Stake in a sanctioned trial.

Back in the fifties a Derby Stake in a sanctioned trial was more or less training. We would repeat the tests that the dog had difficulty in grasping and the ribbons were secondary. Punishing a dog for malfeasance was permissible within reason, too. But today all of that has changed. The sanctioned trials are almost as holy as the licensed trials, and strict decorum must be followed. One chance is permitted for each test, with a minimum of two. To any of you who are fortunate enough to have a dog that you think might make it to Open competition, my advice is this: inform the field trial marshal and the judges that you are not running for the ribbons, but that you wish to train your dog under field trial conditions. If you do this in advance, they just might permit you to correct your dog when he makes a mistake. This is the way to approach sanctioned field trials—not with the desire for ribbons, but with the idea of training your dog. I did this with one of my first dogs and came home with several ribbons, but my first idea was still training.

Even when I judged sanctioned trials where the judge was permitted to run his own dogs, I always set up tests in which my dogs were poor and could use the work. Unfortunately, I have seen many judges who would do just the opposite and set up tests in which their dogs excelled and would win. However, their dogs did not get any training and a ribbon from a sanctioned trial didn't get them very far. Let me tell you a story about how a real Open Stake in a sanctioned trial was run many years ago.

The judges were Lew Pierson, one of the really great judges of a bygone era, and Ray Staudinger, who has forgotten more about Retrievers than most of the present-day handlers know.

Nineteen dogs were entered in the Open All-Age Stakes, and fifteen of them were field trial champions. My young dog was just out of Derby competition and had much to learn. He was the number one dog and did what I thought was a creditable job on a long single retrieve. Ray and Lew thought otherwise. They made me repeat the test four more times, until my young dog pinpointed the shot bird from two hundred yards away. The trial went on for five series and late into the afternoon. When it was over, four dogs placed and one was awarded a Judges' Award of Merit (J.A.M.). All

four places went to field trial champions and my young Chesapeake took the Judges' Award of Merit. I have always been prouder of that ribbon than of many later licensed trial wins. Besides gaining the ribbon, my dog took four giant steps toward Open All-Age competition and maturity.

Now let us consider the sketches of a couple of Derby tests. In the first one we have a one hundred twenty yard single retrieve on land. If you have drilled your dog on doubles, he just might not mark the first bird well, so this single retrieve is a good one to work on. Even though it is in light cover, the mark is long, and unless your Chessie is an exceptional marker, he might mark short.

"BB" in our diagrams designates "Bird Box." This is where the live birds are kept before being thrown and shot. If your dog shows any interest in it, discourage him immediately. This is a "no-no," at least for field trials. If dead birds are used, they usually are carried in a burlap bag. Your dog should be discouraged from showing any interest in it, also.

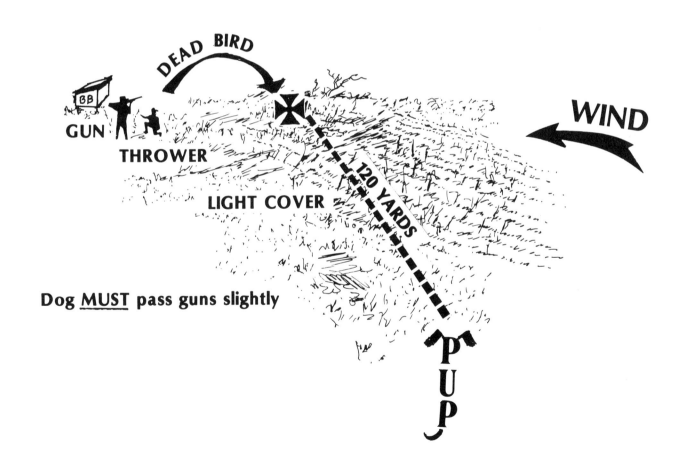

Derby Test—Single Retrieve

Field Champion and Amateur Field Champion Mount Joy's Louistoo. Louis is the only Chesapeake to win two "double-headers" in all-breed competition.

Because a Derby-age Chesapeake is expected to do a double retrieve also, the next sketch shows a double retrieve on land. You will note that the bird (dead) for the long retrieve is thrown first, about ninety yards out—a good long mark. Then the second bird, a live one, is shot, just a bit to the right of the line. Naturally, your Chessie will go to the shot bird first. In the excitement, he just might tend to forget the location of the bird for the long retrieve. This is the purpose of the test. You will note that the wind is blowing from right to left, so give your dog a "line" a bit to the left of the bird. In this way, you can be sure that he is downwind of the bird and has a better chance of winding it and finding it.

Teaching your dog to follow a "line" is not difficult. On land, walk your dog out fifty yards or so and drop the bumper in front of him. Now walk him back to the original starting place. Make your dog sit and face the spot where you dropped the bumper. Now, with your palm open and fingers close together, move your hand and arm forward, literally showing the dog which direction to travel to retrieve the bumper, and give him the command "Back." Remembering the bumper, he most likely will obey your command and retrieve the bumper immediately. If not, then repeat this procedure as often as necessary until he gets the idea. The command "Back"—sending your dog on a "line" or "lining" your dog—will be used later on as part of handling, but this much will suffice for the Derby stage.

"Honoring" is another thing your Chesapeake must learn. It really is very simple. By "honoring," we mean that after working, the dog must move to his handler's left and remain in position without making a motion to retrieve while a second dog retrieves.

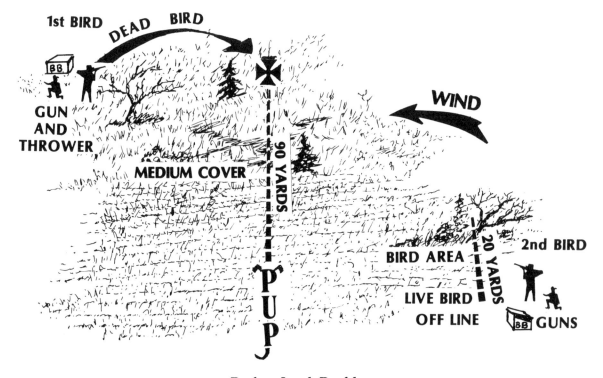

Derby—Land Double

46

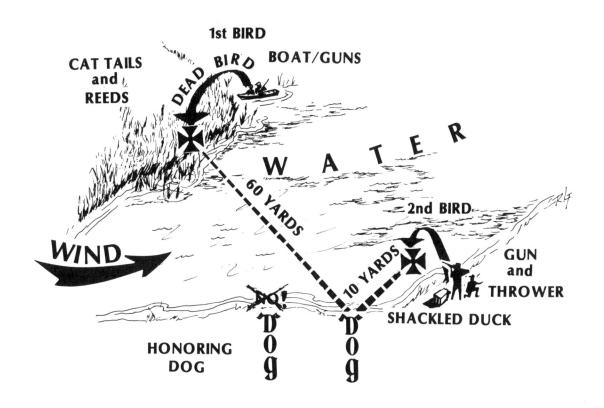

CAT TAILS and REEDS

1st BIRD
BOAT/GUNS
DEAD BIRD

WATER

60 YARDS

2nd BIRD

WIND

10 YARDS

GUN and THROWER

SHACKLED DUCK

NO!

HONORING DOG

DOG

DOG

Qualifying Water Double With Honoring

Look at the sketch above. As you can see, this is a comparatively simple double retrieve, but it provides quite a temptation for the honoring dog to break after the second, or shackled, duck. In the sketch, as you can see, the working dog first makes a retrieve of a quacking mallard at a distance of some ten yards, while the honoring dog just looks on. It is permissible for the honoring dog to stand, but he cannot make a motion toward retrieving or he is OUT. As soon as the working dog is sent for the second bird, the honoring dog and his handler usually are excused, but his handler must wait for the judge to excuse him. Don't just go! As you can see, the proximity of the boat and the Guns might tend to draw the working dog off the mark, especially if he is vague about it. However, if he can count to two and really marks, he should have no trouble.

Now I am going to just touch on training for Open All-Age Stakes, and then leave the rest of the training procedures for the advanced training chapter.

Even in Qualifying or late Derby competition, it will be well for you to teach your Chesapeake to count to three. In other words, to teach him to wait for three birds to be thrown and shot, and to retrieve three birds. The way to do this is the same way you started on double retrieves—only this time you will need three

throwers and Guns and this will entail the help of your group or club.

Have each bird thrower stand out about fifty feet, one on your right, one straight ahead, and one on your left. These positions are somewhat like the positions of the bases on a baseball diamond.

I have always liked to have the bird on the left thrown first, and a bit further out than the other two, then the one from "second base," and then the one on the right. This will send the dog to the right for his first retrieve.

Make sure that all three birds are in plain sight. After your dog delivers the bird on the right, send him for the center one if you are sure that he has seen it. When he (hopefully) retrieves the third bird, act as if you are celebrating New Year's Eve. Your dog will appreciate the praise and will try to do even better.

After your dog has the simple triple retrieve down pat, gradually move the birds further out and then into cover. In the beginning, though, always give your dog at least one bird in plain sight to home in on.

Next, try two birds far out, with the third bird shot right from the line. This will show you how steady your dog is and whether the excitement of that third bird flying right under his nose makes him forget the other two. After you have proven your Chesapeake on this triple retrieve, you may be reasonably sure that he can count to three and that he will sit and wait until you send him out—two very important accomplishments.

Now we go to water retrieving with very much the same procedure. The only difference might be that the Chesapeake likes water so much that he just might break more quickly on water than on land, so be careful. Again use three easy retrieves to start your dog, and then gradually make them harder. When your dog is doing good triple retrieves in water in fairly heavy cover, then, and only then, it is time to shoot the third bird right over his head. He will probably break the first time, but don't worry. That's natural. Just go back to fundamentals for a while and then try again. Eventually your dog will get used to the shot over his head and you will be proud of the way he waits for you to send him. Remember, a Chesapeake that doesn't break occasionally is not worth training. Remember too, you read that here!

After your dog reaches the age of two, he should be able to do a triple retrieve easily, but many dogs are drilled so much on triple and double retrieves that they tend to forget the long, tough, single retrieve. The sketch here shows a situation that would test the mettle of any dog, and if he waits for a second bird, ignore it. Note that first the dog must navigate a stone wall, then heavy cover, then a dirt road. After that he must go through an additional fifty yards of light cover before arriving at the area where the bird has been thrown. A few tests similar to this will bring out your Chesapeake's marking ability.

Now we come to a test of your dog's ability to work a blind retrieve. (That is, one where he does not see the bird fall.) Remember your lessons on lining and you shouldn't have much trouble with this. As you can see, the distance is one hundred twenty yards, which is not long for a blind retrieve on land with no diversions. Your dog must go through a brook about forty yards out and then traverse cover before arriving at the blind. The bird planter is stationed to the right in heavy cover where the dog cannot see or wind him, for the wind is coming from the opposite direction. If your dog starts hunting short, give him a short blast of the whistle. He should sit and look at you. Then give him a loud "BACK," with your hand upright over your head and moving forward. If he goes on far enough, but veers upwind of the bird, then stop him in the same way and bellow "OVER," with your right arm at a right angle to your body and pointing right. Eventually, he should find the bird.

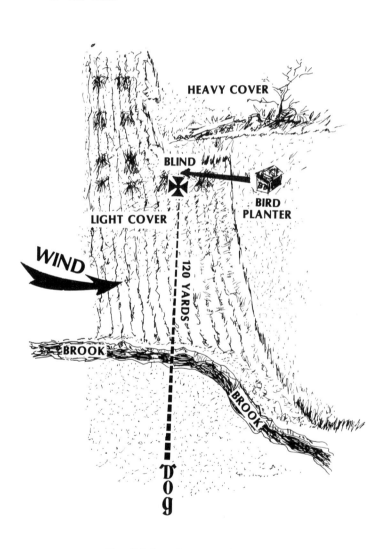

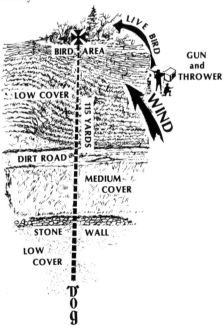

Qualifying Single

Qualifying Land Blind

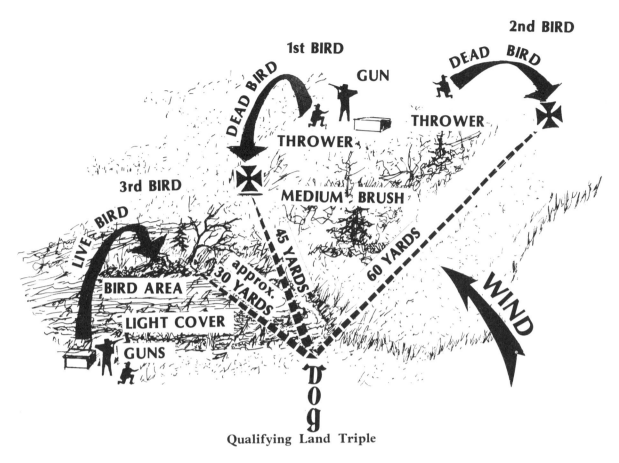

1st BIRD

2nd BIRD

DEAD BIRD

GUN

DEAD BIRD

THROWER

THROWER

3rd BIRD

MEDIUM BRUSH

LIVE BIRD

45 YARDS

approx. 30 YARDS

60 YARDS

BIRD AREA

LIGHT COVER

GUNS

WIND

D o g

Qualifying Land Triple

Below: Mount Joy's Mighty Ike, owned by Helen Fleischmann, makes a successful retrieve.

When your dog reaches the ripe old age of two and is in Qualifying Stakes, he should be able to start on triple retrieves similar to the one shown in the sketch above.

Note that the two dead birds are thrown rather far out—one sixty and the other forty-five yards. Then the "memory-eraser" is a live bird shot closer in. Your dog obviously will go for the live bird first, or he's not a Chesapeake. When he comes in with it, let him choose the next one himself. It will save a lot of heartaches, for the Chesapeake is a very self-willed dog. I always let my Chessies choose their birds. It saves time.

If you have followed my instructions, and if your Chesapeake pup was bred right in the first place, you should have a dog that is performing creditably in Derby Stakes and that is a real pleasure to have around while hunting.

Our chapter on advanced Retriever training is not for everyone. Very few dogs of any Retriever breed, including Chesapeakes, ever run in an Open All-Age Stake. The training is arduous. I write the chapter for two reasons: first, the book would not be complete without it; and second, the fortunate few who have a really talented Chessie pup will benefit greatly by it.

Champion Bayberry Pete, owned by Helen Fleischmann, looks pensive after making a successful retrieve.

Advanced Training for Your Chesapeake Bay Retriever

In the preceding chapter we took up triple retrieves in general. Here we do so in particular.

Here the first triple-retrieve test is on land. Picture heavy cover about fifty yards out to the right and to the left, and light cover more than a hundred yards away down the center. The first bird is dead and is thrown down the center a long, long way. Then a bird to the left is shot some fifty yards out. Third, a bird is thrown in the air right over your dog and either you or the Gun shoots it to drop some fifteen or twenty feet from the line. Now your dog is very excited about that third bird falling almost at his feet. Can he remember the other two? If he can, he's better than most dogs running in Open All-Age Stakes. If he can remember them with help from his handler, he is above average. This is why it is so important for you to mark the birds. If the handler doesn't mark them and his Chesapeake doesn't mark them, then who does?

Say your dog dashes out and retrieves the flyer. Then he takes a fair line and, with a good nose, comes up with the second bird. You know he has forgotten the third. What to do! Line him very carefully, as if this were a blind retrieve. Take your time and then send him. If he goes far enough on the line, and your line is a good one, he should come back triumphantly with the bird. If he wavers and seems unsure, handle him immediately. Don't wait for him to hunt. Judges will take off more points for a dog that just runs around in a confused manner than for one that requires handling but goes out smartly and returns with the bird. This is just one of the problems you will encounter in advanced training.

I have gone into lining a great deal, but into actual handling, very little. You have been taught how to make

The Chesapeake retrieves eagerly in any season and despite the most adverse weather conditions.

Icy water and deep snow do not deter this Chesapeake as he sets out in response to his handler's command.

your dog sit immediately when you signal him with one short whistle blast. Here is how to handle your dog to good effect.

Go back to your "baseball diamond" pattern. Use the three boat bumpers—one at each of the "bases," first, second, and third. Now send your dog to the "pitcher's mound" and stop him with that one whistle blast. If he has been trained correctly, he will sit immediately and look at you. Now stand up straight, extend your left arm and holler "OVER." Since there are bumpers at all three stations, your Chessie probably will go to your left and pick up the bumper at "third base." Whistle him in. Repeat this with the other two bumpers. And then go through the entire procedure enough times on different days so that your dog really knows what you mean. Now you are ready to handle him longer distances and gradually to increase the cover through which you send him to retrieve.

If your Chessie is a mature dog, about two weeks of handling training should make him reasonably tractable. In my experience, Chesapeakes will take a line forever, or until they are stopped. A Chesapeake is not easy to stop at a distance, and after he stops, it is problematical as to whether he follows your direction signal if his mind does not agree with yours. Some people undoubtedly will disagree with me, but this has been my experience with Chesapeakes. A Chessie really has a mind of his own.

On the other hand, if you give your dog a signal into very heavy cover and let him search as he pleases, your Chesapeake undoubtedly will find the bird if it is there, while other breeds would quit in disgust. This sets the Chessie apart. If there is a cripple that the judges do not see (a cripple or "runner" usually doesn't count as a successful retrieve in field trials), your Chessie will track it down in no time but, unfortunately, probably will receive no credit for the feat. But he won't care as long as his owner-handler gives him his just due. Again, this is the Chesapeake.

51

Left: Bob Massaroni cautions his Chesapeake to remain still as they wait for the ducks to land.

Right: The ducks have landed, but Spinner waits for his handler to shoot and then give the command to retrieve.

Left: The Chessie responds eagerly to his handler's command to retrieve.

"Good Boy!"

Left: The Chessie and his handler demonstrate the way to practice entering a boat.

Right: The handler positions his Chessie in the boat by giving the "Stay" command.

54

Training Your Chesapeake for Hunting

Although I have devoted many pages to telling you how to train your Chesapeake for field trials, I have not yet touched on how to train him for hunting under actual field conditions. Because the Chesapeake is becoming more and more a hunting companion and less and less a competitive field trial dog, it behooves me to tell you about training for situations that never come up in field trials but occur time and again in hunting.

One of the main problems that I have encountered in hunting with Chesapeakes trained purely for field trials, is their inability to get into or out of a boat, and to stay in one once the boat starts to rock a bit. Again, this is training that you may provide as soon as your dog starts hunting with you, at about one year of age.

For training aids you will need a light aluminum boat of the type that most hunters use. To avoid excessive ducking for the trainer, I would advise that the preliminary training be done on land, using the boat with a few small logs under it to simulate the roll or unsteadiness usually experienced when in a boat that is on water.

When the boat is in position, step into it slowly, with your dog heeling at your side. When you stop, he will sit, if he has learned his obedience commands. When he sits, position him the way you want him to remain, and tell him to stay. Now, using your feet and shifting your weight from side to side, rock the boat a bit. If your dog shows any tendency to jump out, keep repeating the command "Stay." If he jumps out of the boat the first few times—which he probably will—repeat the whole procedure until he will stay in the boat where you put him.

The reason I recommend starting with a rolling boat rather than one on calm water is simple. When your dog actually enters a boat that is on water, the boat surely will rock even if the water is calm, and if your dog doesn't know what to do, both dog and handler are likely to get a ducking.

You also can teach your Chesapeake to get in a boat by using the command "Kennel," which I assume you already have taught him means that he is to enter his crate, a particular room, or anywhere else you want him to go. If this command has been inculcated in your Chesapeake's training correctly, he automatically will respond to it, no matter what the situation. It also is important, once your dog is in the boat, that you position him correctly so that the boat doesn't tip when you are shooting, either when you are alone or when you are with a companion.

I remember the story of an actual happening that is a perfect example of what will occur if the occupants of a boat are not positioned properly. Three obviously novice duck hunters were in a boat, all with 12 gauge duck guns. All three were facing in the same direction when a lone duck flew over. All three fired at the same time—and there were three very wet duck hunters.

The moral of this is, if you are hunting alone with just your dog, position him at the stern, with you toward the other end, or at least in the middle. If you have a companion, the two of you should sit back to back in the middle of the boat with the Chesapeake at the stern.

Now that your Chessie has mastered the first steps of boating, let's put his abilities to practical use, but still in a training stage.

You will need a helper, who will remain on land during the early phases of this training, and either some birds or some bumpers which your helper will throw for your dog to retrieve.

We now have our boat, some paddles, and your Chesapeake on the edge of some water. Even a small cow pond will do. First give your Chessie the command "Kennel." When he is safely in the boat and sitting quietly, you get in. I assume that you have your 12 gauge shotgun with you, and that you also have some "popper" shells for training. These are shells with powder and wads, but no pellets. They are much safer than live ammunition, and they have less recoil, rocking the boat hardly at all when you fire. These are important factors when you also are concentrating on training your dog.

Have your helper, who is standing on land, throw a bird or bumper into the middle of the water in plain sight of the dog. Remember this is not a retrieving lesson primarily, but rather a lesson to teach your dog to get into and out of your boat correctly. Give your dog the command to retrieve. If he is sitting in the stern of the boat facing the open water as he should be, he will dive off the stern and swim for the bird. Try to make him return to the stern of the boat. When he does, first take the bird from his mouth, then help him into the boat. You will get slightly damp, but this is where the Chesapeake excels. He sheds water like a duck. Even after he has made several retrieves, you will find, if you rub his coat the wrong way, that he is still bone dry underneath.

The final step in this phase of your dog's training should take place in the middle of the pond or stream. Using the same commands, paddle out a ways and put down a light anchor. Have your helper throw the bird, preferably from land, and then fire with your popper shell. Now remember, always have your dog at the stern of the boat. Send him from there and make him return there. You will learn to help him into the boat quite easily and he will learn to help you.

One thing I have never been able to teach my Chesapeakes upon their return to my boat is NOT TO SHAKE! I hope you have better luck. Once your dog has mastered the techniques of getting out of and back into the boat, you will be surprised at how much fun it is hunting with him in swamps and marshes that you can enter only by boat. Your hunting also will be much more productive when you use a Chesapeake.

Let us turn now to teaching your Chesapeake not to play with decoy rigs or get inside them. By a decoy rig, I mean ten or more decoys anchored singly, attached by bars, or, as is most common, attached by cord or string. I use a dozen decoys with the latter arrangement.

Although most field trial dogs know enough not to pick up a decoy, very few field trial dogs know much about decoy rigs, for they are not used in field trials.

The first step is to put the rig out on bare ground, set up the same way it would be in water. Now walk your Chesapeake around the decoy rig. When he bends down to sniff the decoys, pull up on his choke collar with a sharp "NO!" When he attempts to step inside the decoy rig, yank him back, again with the "NO" command. Within a few days it should be firmly fixed in his mind that he is not to pick up a decoy, and that he is to stay outside the rig. Now we come to the acid test.

Set out in the water four decoys strung together as I have described. From the shore, throw a live, shackled duck into the middle of the rig. Do not send your dog yet. When the duck has struggled to the edge of the decoy rig, send your dog. If he retrieves it correctly, be lavish in your praise. If he comes back with your decoys around his neck and various other portions of his anatomy, do not correct him. Just repeat, and repeat until he gets it right. After a while he will understand just what is expected of him and will wait for his bird patiently. I have seen a ten-month-old Chessie pup master this in just a few weeks, so don't despair. Patience is the name of the game.

If your Chessie does not respond quickly to this phase of training, you might try throwing the birds outside the rig until he learns not to enter it. Once he understands that he is not to go inside your rig, the problem is solved.

Now let us discuss some of the more advanced types of training for hunting. Remember that your dog must master all of the rudimentary obedience commands discussed in the chapter on early training before you can be successful at this.

First let us discuss jump shooting. Much of this type of hunting is done flat on your stomach with your Chessie in the same position. A Chesapeake will learn to crawl very easily.

Let me cite an example of one type of jump shooting. One morning I arrived at my favorite pond together with my favorite Chesapeake, and we reconnoitered the area to find out, before we were seen, whether there were any unsuspecting ducks or geese on the water.

This entailed crawling on my belly for one hundred yards through the grass and reeds, and, more important, having my dog crawl with me. Yes, I mean my dog, as well as I, had to stay out of sight, because any motion would spook any ducks that might be there.

This particular morning, there were three black ducks on the water. Because my dog and I were crawling, we managed to get within forty yards or so before the ducks spotted us. As they turned to take off, I managed to bring one down on the fly. They were travelling so fast that I didn't even bother to snap off a second shot.

The crawling proved fruitful. I had a duck dinner and my young Chessie had the pleasure of a retrieve before the day even started.

Teaching your Chesapeake to crawl is easier than it sounds, especially since most Chessies are natural clowns and like to imitate their masters. When you start this phase of training, make sure that you always have a helper at the pond to throw a duck onto the water when you finally leap to your feet and shoot. A reward is important and shows your Chessie that he is doing what you want him to do. Now get to a spot with plenty of tall reeds and get down on your stomach. From the prone position, call your dog softly and give him the command "Down." He probably will lie down alongside you and look at you as if he thinks you have gone out of your mind. Mine always gave me a big grin, for a Chessie and a grin are synonomous.

Now start crawling, and give your dog a forward hand signal. If he gets up, stop, give him the command "Down," and try again. Usually within a comparatively short period of time, a week or so, he will catch on.

When you have finally managed, together with your Chesapeake, to crawl almost to the water, give your helper the signal to throw the bird, and then you jump up and bang away. Almost immediately give your Chessie the signal to retrieve. When he brings the bird to you, it will dawn on him what this is all about and you'll have very little trouble from then on.

If your Chessie is two years old or older and has had some experience in hunting ducks, he will learn this lesson quickly. If he is much older, then it might take a bit longer, but eventually he'll do it. The Chesapeake is not the most tractable Retriever, in my opinion, but Chesapeakes prove themselves to be the smartest as soon as they understand the "why" of doing things.

Before you actually try jump shooting on wild game, be sure to dirty up the outside of your gun barrel— using something that will not damage the barrel. If the barrel is shiny, it is capable of giving off a telltale glint that will spook the birds.

Another type of jump shooting might interest you after your Chesapeake has had a season or two of experience in duck hunting. Remember, I just told you that the Chesapeake is the smartest Retriever. Well, the following is an extreme example of Chesapeake intelligence, but it's true.

My wife and I once had a Chesapeake that we used to drive waterbound ducks or geese in toward us. By waterbound, I mean that the birds were swimming in the middle of a large pond and would not venture near enough either for a shot or so that they could be scared into taking off.

With my wife and me concealed, one on each side of the birds, our Chessie would enter the water from the opposite shore and swim leisurely out toward the birds. If he was nonchalant enough about it, the birds would just keep swimming away from him and, of course, toward my wife and me. Now comes the "fun part." When we thought the birds were close enough, we both arose suddenly. When the birds saw us, they literally panicked. There was a large dog behind them and two human gunners, one on each side of them. Sometimes the ducks would flare to one side or the other and either my wife or I would have at least two. About fifty percent of the time the ducks would try to plow between

the two gunners and then, being careful not to shoot too low, we really had a field day. In all my years of shooting, I have never seen the ducks flare back over the dog, which, of course, is their only safe route.

Even if we wounded a few, they would be "duck soup" for our big Chessie to scoop out of the water.

Again it is hard actually to train your Chesapeake to herd ducks, but many Chessies have the native ability and will know instinctively what you want them to do. Be sure your Chessie is not too young when you try this type of hunting, though.

Another somewhat easier method of jump shooting is to have your Chesapeake stay in one position or in one spot while you continue crawling. I use this method when the ducks, or especially geese, are very wary, and any movement might spook them.

When my Chessie and I have crawled a certain distance and I want to swing around to a different position, I either whisper "Stay" to him or give him the hand signal. Again, this presupposes that your Chesapeake knows his obedience commands. They are important.

Then I continue crawling to where I want to go while my "big stoop" keeps one eye on the quarry and the other on me, although from his original position.

Bob Massoroni with his dogs, concealed in the cornfield as they wait for the game to come within range.

Chessie and handler wait patiently as they anticipate a second successful retrieve.

The moment I stand up, he does likewise, to mark the birds better. He doesn't need any command for this. When I am finished shooting, he goes at the wave of my arm or with the command "Back," and retrieves to hand. If I miss, he sometimes won't speak to me for a week! Seriously, the Chesapeake is quite sensitive about his hunting. He is excellent at his job, and he expects you to be at least reasonably accurate at yours.

One morning when I was shooting from too much distance, or misjudging the killing power of the new steel ammunition, I had missed six clean shots. Suddenly, without warning, my Chessie took off from my side. At first I thought he had spotted something that I had wounded, but alas, this was not the case. Upon returning some time later to my wagon, I found my big Chessie curled up in his comfortable crate, sound asleep. He could think of no better way of telling me what he thought of me and my shooting expertise. Instead of chastening him, I felt as if I should apologize. Again, this is the true Chesapeake. When you take him hunting, you had just better hit something.

One more word of advice before moving on to shooting from blinds. This advice entails gun safety and is very important both for your own safety and for that of your Chesapeake as well as anyone hunting with you.

When you crawl, always have the safety on with the gun across your arms and the barrel pointing in a safe direction. By safe direction, I mean if your dog or hunting partner or both are on your left, the gun barrel should point right, and vice versa. Having the gun crossways definitely gives more leverage for crawling and cuts the chance of injury to anyone in case of an accidental discharge.

Now let's take up shooting from a blind, both a stationary blind and a floating blind. This is another facet of waterfowl hunting at which the Chesapeake excels. As I go on, you will understand why.

By blinds, I don't mean those big ones down in Maryland. To me, shooting from one of those is too much like shooting ducks in a barrel. The ducks and geese fly over, heading for their home in one of the preserves, and the blind (for $50 or more a day) is usually located just outside of the preserve. I won't subject my Chessies to the indignity of this simple retrieving. In fact, if I were to attempt to do so, I wouldn't be surprised if they just went back to my car and let me retrieve my own birds. A Chessie wants a challenge.

No, the blinds that I am going to tell you about are ones that you can build yourself, with materials right on the scene, except for the floats. In fact, you almost have to build the blinds with material from right where you plan to shoot, for they won't look natural otherwise.

First, let's take the stationary blind. This is usually built along the shore of a lake or pond that you know harbors ducks.

My wife and I like to build in the early spring as soon as the ice breaks. This gives us a chance to bring our Chessies along and get them accustomed to the location as well as acclimate the young dogs to the water. It also, of course, gives the birds a chance to get used to seeing the blind on their pond.

A few years ago we built a dandy at a lake that was almost inaccessible to anyone without a four-wheel-drive vehicle or a good pair of legs. We usually check our blinds every week or so, but somehow we neglected this one for over a month, or maybe even longer. When we finally arrived and peered inside, there were two hen mallards, one on each side. You guessed it, they were nesting. Believe it or not, with just one command to "leave it," the young Chesapeake we had with us paid no more attention to the two birds.

Some weeks later we had the pleasure of seeing one of the hens lead a brood of eight ducklings out into the water. The other obviously had gone before. I have seen this sight many times both in the wild and at our own ponds, but it never fails to excite me. Mother Nature is really versatile, and that's one use for a good blind!

We usually build our blinds with a frame of light birch or any other saplings that are available. And we make each blind big enough for two people and one Chesapeake. (When you make yours, be sure you have a good space for your Chessie so the concussion from the gun doesn't deafen him.) We use just one Chessie in the blind. If we have two along, the other one, usually the older one, sits outside at a good vantage point to mark the birds as they fall. Remember, a Chessie, no matter what the color of his coat may be, won't spook birds, but make sure there are no choke chains or other shiny objects on him, for anything that reflects the light will spook them.

The covering for the blind should be native to the area so it will blend in with the scenery. If there are lots of reeds around, use reeds. If dead grass predominates, use that. Just make sure that, to your eye, the blind blends into the surroundings as well as possible. By the time the duck season rolls around, the resident ducks will accept the blind as part of their environment, and they will be very helpful in drawing in the migrating flocks. These migrants, of course, are what you want for your dinner. Leave the residents alone as much as possible and teach your Chesapeake to do the same. You'll be surprised how very quickly your Chessie will learn this lesson.

When constructing your blind, remember to have your entrance on dry land. If it's in tidal water, build far enough back to ensure that you will have a dry entrance. Be settled in your blind before daybreak, along with your Chesapeake, and make a minimum of fuss getting settled. Again, you'll be pleasantly surprised at your Chesapeake. As boisterous as he is in other situations, he'll be practically noiseless in shooting territory.

I like my blinds to be simple, but you can make yours as elaborate as you wish. I have hunted from some homemade blinds that had potbellied stoves and foot warmers. One even had a portable bar—for use after the hunting, of course.

You don't necessarily have to construct your blind at water. Some years back we had fairly large flocks of Canada geese, on which the Chesapeake excels. The geese were landing in a neighborhood farmer's cornfield. We obtained permission from the farmer to build a blind, largely with the cornhusks.

The first year was unproductive, although it taught our young Chesapeakes how to hunt in a cornfield. They kicked up quite a few pheasants, which were a bonus, for the pheasant season overlapped the waterfowl season.

The farmer was kind enough to plant around the blind and let it stand for the second season, and that's when we reaped a bonanza. The first year, the geese were spooked because the blind was something new. But when they saw it the second year, they accepted it as part of their environment. By the way, it is true that if you are lucky and shoot down the flock leader, the remainder of the flock will mill about for several minutes before they regroup. You can get in some good shooting and your Chesapeake will have some good retrieving.

The land blind may be built of sturdy material that is light enough to be transported from field to field. Because most of the fields in which geese land contain corn, a blind that blends into the surroundings in one field will blend into the scenery in any of them.   We often have moved from field to field along with our Chesapeakes, sometimes getting to a field just ten minutes ahead of a flight. It's fun!

The Chesapeake isn't the only good goose dog, but he is by far the best. Our Chessies have utterly no fear of any bird, although many other Retrievers will back off when the wounded goose starts flapping those lethal wings. Not so the Chessie. He circles warily and then dives in for a hold on the neck when there's an opening. One good clamping hold and that is the end of Mr. or Mrs. Goose.

Also, the Chesapeake, having a very strong neck and excellent mouth, has no trouble handling this bird that averages from nine to eleven pounds in weight, with some even larger. The Chesapeake carries a goose as if it were a pigeon. Their weight is the main reason that geese are not used in the trials.

Now let me tell you something about floating blinds and the equipment that you'll need. First of all, you'll need something besides the blind to lure the flights down, so invest in at least a small rig of decoys, perhaps a half dozen or so. In fact, if you hunt with friends and share the cost of building the blind, each of you could donate a half dozen decoys, and you will then have a rig that is more than respectable.

The first thing to think of in planning for a floating blind is the flotation. You can buy an expensive floating dock, or you can tie together four or six old oil drums, depending on their size, and cover them with light but strong planking. Again your roof and sides should have a lightweight frame and be covered with the same vegetation that exists along the shore of your lake, pond, or waterway.

I prefer a three-sided blind with open shooting from the front so that my Chesapeake can mark, and I cut slits on both sides for shooting from the sides. The slits must be large enough for the hunter to see the birds, but for the Chesapeake, this, of course, will be the blind retrieving at which he excels. I frown upon a potbellied stove or other form of heating equipment. First, the Chessie likes the cold and doesn't like the heat. Next, there is too much chance of fire and the resultant cold bath.

I assume you will be shooting with at least one other person and two Chessies, so here is another very important item for your blind. While your dogs can launch themselves easily into the water, they will have great difficulty in returning unless you make special provisions for them. Therefore, you should build a slotted ramp at the front of the blind. This should be braced from about two feet under the water and should slant gradually up to the front of the blind. Then the Chessies will be able to deliver the birds without difficulty.

If you plan to have one of your Chesapeakes sitting outside the blind, you will need to build a platform (one that is easily accessible) on one side of the blind and then teach the Chessie to sit on it. This is done very easily, but if your Chessie seems a bit uneasy on his perch, have your partner throw a few pigeons up, shoot them, and have your Chessie retrieve them from the platform. Before long you will find that he returns to the platform of his own volition. Chesapeakes are smart—make no mistake about that.

Before leaving you to the happiness of hunting with your Chesapeake, here is a word of caution about building land blinds. If possible, avoid building your land blind in a field where cattle or horses are kept. Otherwise, you may arrive some morning for a day of shooting only to find a nice frame with the camouflage neatly devoured by your bovine or equine friends.

Anyhow, good hunting for you and your Chesapeake!

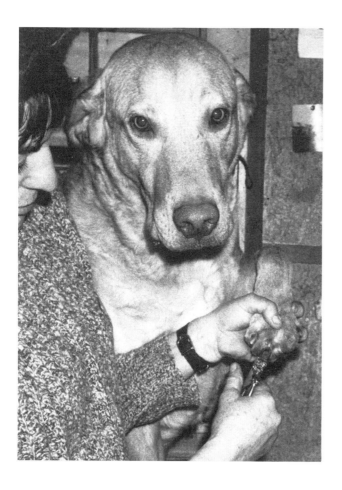

With Spinner's assistance, Ruth Williams Beaman demonstrates correct procedures for grooming the Chesapeake for the show ring. At left and below, she is trimming the dog's nails, being careful not to clip back into the quick. (All grooming photos by Bob Massaroni.)

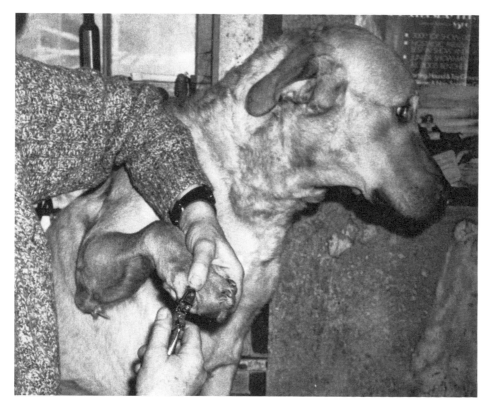

Preparation for the Show Ring

By Ruth Williams Beaman

Author's note: I first wrote this chapter myself, but I wasn't satisfied with it. Although I enjoyed a modicum of success as a professional handler of Sporting Dogs, my wife was much better than I. Ruth was probably the world's leading handler of Sporting Dogs in the late fifties and during most of the sixties. During that time she also handled more Chesapeakes professionally than any other professional handler—and with a great deal of success. So, it is with a sigh of relief that I turn this chapter over to someone who really knows: Ruth Williams Beaman.

If you are lucky enough to have a young pup that you plan to show, and if he has promise of really good conformation, start right now to train him for the show ring!

This can be done at the same time your pup is being leash trained, house trained, started in the field, and started in obedience.

With our litters, we inspect each pup daily from birth, so all are well accustomed to handling by the time they reach the age of six weeks. When your Chessie's little legs will hold him (or her) up, he (or she) should be positioned in a show pose, known as "stacking," for the daily examination. If your pup has not been examined each day when you acquire him, this is where you start, no matter what the pup's age may be.

First make sure that all essential medical attention has been provided by your veterinarian. This will include all inoculations, a stool check for worms and any worming that may be necessary, and a checkup for general health.

If your Chessie is very young (under three months), any sturdy table or bench can be used for the daily examination. If you are training an older pup or even a mature Chesapeake, use a VERY sturdy low bench—one that has a top about eighteen inches from the floor.

A mat or a piece of carpeting should be glued or tacked to the top surface of the bench in order to provide safe footing for the dog. This bench will be useful not only for training the dog to stand in the show pose, but also for grooming him, which will be discussed a little later.

If you are going to build the bench yourself, make the top approximately 24" x 36". This is so that you can work from all sides of your Chessie, even after he attains full growth.

Teach your youngster or adult to stand in a show pose on the bench. Position his front legs so that they look straight from both sides as well as from the front. The rear legs will be correct if, when viewing the dog from behind, you place them just a little wider than the front legs. The hind leg position will be correct if the legs are set so that from side views they are in a straight line from hock to foot. Now, when your Chessie will stay in this position on the bench with your hand only, on his muzzle, start giving him the command "Stand—Stay!" Repeat this daily. Be sure your Chessie's legs stay in the position that you put them in. Once he has learned to leave his feet where you put them, you may want to alter his stance somewhat, according to his structure.

All right, now give the command "Stand—Stay," and leave your Chessie on his own on the bench without using your hands to control him. Walk completely around your dog. Now go back to his head. Then walk away and remain standing where the dog can see you, but at least ten feet away from him.

When you can do this successfully, have some of your friends walk up to the dog and around him. The first few times you attempt this, you undoubtedly will find it necessary to remain at your Chessie's head and perhaps reset his stance, for he may break because of the excitement of new admirers. The dog must be steady to being handled from his head back to his tail, from either side, and from back to front. When this has been accomplished, the entire procedure must be repeated with many different distractions. Parking lots in supermarkets with many people moving about would be my choice of good practice areas. The pup must learn to "stack" on any type of surface, from your bench to grass to wooden floors.

I would hope that by this time you will have trained your Chessie to the leash, but if you haven't, here is what you do. Put a heavy leather collar (not a "choke collar") on your Chessie, and tie him to a solid object, using a heavy leash or a sturdy rope. In the event that he becomes entangled, he will not hurt himself as he might if he were held fast by a chain. Most Chessie pups will fight for a few minutes, and then realize that they are tied fast. They will then give up the struggle and wait for you to return and release them.

When this point is reached, return to your pup with your walking leash in hand, snap it to the collar ring, and unfasten the rope. The pup will then think he is free to play, only to find that he must obey the leash you have in your hand. Play with your pup, teasing him to come along with you until he finds that he can only go so far before he has to walk with you. At this point, change to a chain or nylon choke collar and continue with the training for the show ring which will be described in chapters which follow. Your dog is now ready for you and he (or she) to learn to show together.

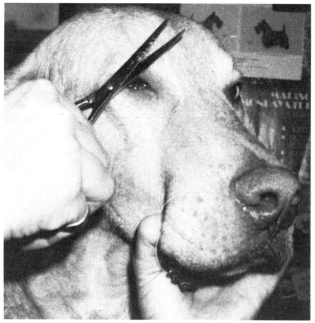

Above: Trimming around the eyes. Novices should be sure to use blunt-tipped scissors to avoid injury to the dog.

Below: Trimming the lashes. (This is done for both show and field, for the lashes tend to grow into the eye.)

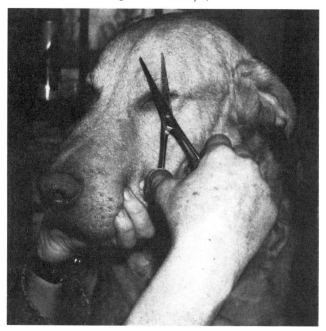

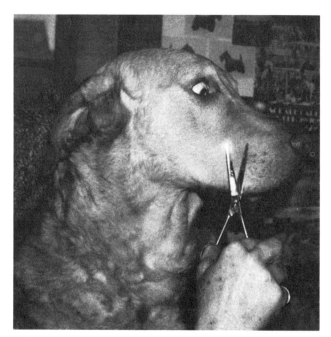

Above: Trimming the whiskers, taking care not to injure or frighten the dog, and again using blunt-tipped scissors.

Below: Cleaning the ears. Be sure you do not go too deeply into the ear canal. If there is evidence of infection or a bad odor, consult your veterinarian.

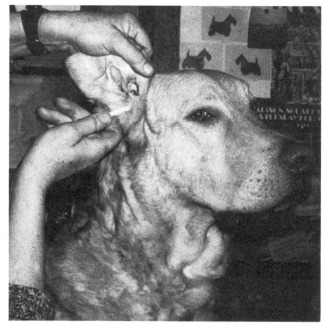

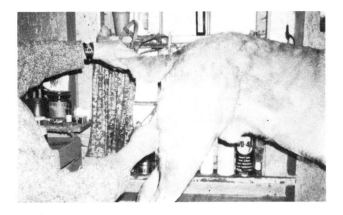

Left: Taking the long hairs off the rear. Do not overdo this. Take off just enough to make the dog pleasing to the eye of the judge.

Right: Snipping the hair on the end of the tail to make it even in length. Again, don't overdo it.

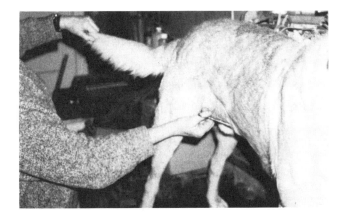

Left: Trimming to even the hair on the underside of the dog. Here, too, be sure you don't overdo it.

Right: Combing the leg coat.

Above: Ruth Williams Beaman checks the tail and hindquarters for proper positioning as she places the Chessie in show stance.

Above: Now she coaxes the Chessie into holding his head in the proper position.

Below: Both front and rear are now properly positioned.

Below: The Chesapeake stands regally, perfectly groomed and in perfect show stance.

How to Show the Chesapeake

In order to become a champion, a dog must win fifteen points in bench-show competition. These fifteen points must include points from at least two major wins—that is, at least two shows where three or more points are awarded. The major wins must be under two different judges, and one or more of the remaining points must be won under a third judge. The most points ever awarded at a show is five and the least is one, so, in order to become a champion, a dog must be exhibited and must win at least three shows—and usually he is shown many times before he wins his championship.

The Chesapeake Bay Retriever is one of the easiest breeds to show if the dog has been selected wisely, brought up correctly, and trained to perform in the show ring.

When, however, an ignorant owner attempts to take a dog to even a match show when the dog has been protected in the house, has been coddled and spoiled, and has not been trained, catastrophic results well might ensue. Let me give you an example.

Some years back I was judging the Chesapeake classes at a large match show. One proud owner hauled his ninety pound specimen into the ring and the circus started. The Chessie dragged the owner from one dog to another, trying to fight. When I attempted to intervene, the dog was perfectly willing to take me on too. I was not amused. I dismissed the recalcitrant dog and ignorant owner from the ring without a ribbon, even though there were only two other dogs in his class. I asked the owner to wait for my explanation, but he walked out in a huff, and probably never attended a dog show again.

So in this chapter on how to show a Chesapeake, I am going to take you through all the various steps that are necessary to prepare your Chesapeake for the show ring correctly.

The first step obviously is the selection of the pup. After reading books on the subject and studying the breed Standard, please go to a reputable breeder. Tell the breeder that you want a dog primarily to show. This can be a breeder of either show or field dogs, for in the Chesapeake breed the two are not separated as they are in some of the other Sporting breeds. Study pedigrees of pups that are available, and whenever you see a pedigree listing several dogs whose names are preceded by "Ch.," which means the dog earned a championship title in bench competition, or "Dual Ch.," which means the dog earned titles in both bench and field competition, become interested in the pups.

You may have to pay a bit more, but, believe me, it is worth it. There is no average price for a good dog, but most breeders will charge less when they know the dog is going to compete either in the field or on the bench.

Now you have your pup and have dutifully trotted him over to your friendly veterinarian for inoculations. At the same time, have your vet check a stool sample for worms. It will save you much worry later on.

After your pup has been fully immunized and reasonably well house trained, start introducing him to people. Following the instructions in the preceding chapter, teach him to walk on a leash and a choke collar without a fuss, and take him with you any place that dogs are permitted. At the tender age of four months you may start his preliminary obedience training. Try to find an obedience training course in your area and enroll him in it. Again, this exposure to other dogs will prove invaluable later on.

At this young age, your pup should not be forced, but he can readily assimilate the following commands: Heel, Stand, Sit, and Come. You will notice that I put "Stand" before "Sit." This is so he will be sure to know both and will not constantly be sitting when you take him in the show ring. The commands also will give you control over your dog, even while he is young. This is very important, especially with a Chesapeake. I don't say that all Chessies are fighters, but it is better to have your dog under control at an early age so the problem does not occur.

Now let us assume that your Chesapeake has reached six months of age, this being the earliest age at which he can be shown. He should know how to walk or trot at your side without raising undue commotion. He should know how to sit quietly at your side when you stop. He also should know that he should stand when you give him the command. These are the only commands he will need to know for the show ring.

The Chesapeake is shown more *au naturel* than almost any of the other Sporting breeds. Keep your Chessie's toenails cut back to neaten his feet. (This is another thing that should be started at an early age so that he will become accustomed to it.) As a general rule a bath is not necessary unless your dog is shedding. Then bathe him a day or two before the show and brush out the dead hair vigorously with a wire brush. If you want to do so, you may take your Chessie swimming in a clean lake or pond, let him dry naturally, and then use the brush. You will notice that I didn't say "in warm weather." This does not apply to Chesapeakes that have become accustomed to going into ponds or streams. Anywhere the water is not frozen, or where the dog can break the ice, will suffice.

Now is the time for you to visit a few shows, without your dog, just to get the idea of how the Chesapeakes are shown. There are match shows in most areas. These are shows that do not give championship points, but they can be an important means of getting your dog accustomed to the show ring.

Enter your Chessie in several match shows and soon he will virtually set himself up when you give the command "Stand." Most intelligent Chessies love to show off, and yours will be no exception. Make sure that he will walk along with you or trot along with you on a loose leash. This means that he is not pulling or tugging, and it is especially important with Chesapeakes, for they tend not to show themselves to best advantage when they are held on a tight leash.

At match shows as well as at licensed dog shows, the class will assemble in the ring, and then the judge will ask that the dogs be paraded in line, moving counter-clockwise in a circle. If you have trained your Chessie well, you will have no difficulty controlling him in the ring, where he must change pace quickly and gracefully and walk and trot elegantly and proudly with head erect. The show dog must also stand quietly for inspection, posing like a statue for several minutes while the judge observes his structure in detail, examines his teeth, feet, coat, etc.

As the judge examines the class, he measures each dog against the ideal described in the breed Standard, then measures the dogs against each other in a comparative sense and selects for first place the Chessie that comes closest to conforming to the Chesapeake Standard.

Now that you think you're ready for it, let's go to a licensed dog show giving championship points. As I told you in the chapter on early training for the Chesapeake, one of the first commands to teach your Chessie is "Kennel" or "Crate." If he has learned this command, it will save you untold agony when you bring him to his first show nicely ensconced in his crate.

Each breed is shown at a definite time in a definite ring. As soon as you arrive at the show, check to make sure of the exact location of the ring where you are to show your dog, and the time you and he are to be there. About fifteen minutes before your dog is to be shown, take him out of the crate and exercise him. I assume, of course, that he has become accustomed to the hustle and bustle of a show through his match show experience. If he has not, then walk him around for about half an hour, but make sure that he does not become hot or bored, especially at shows during the warmer months. Go to the steward in your ring and ask for your number. The number will be the same as that on the identification slip that you received when you sent in your entry. Put the arm band bearing this number on your left arm, and you are ready to go.

One Chesapeake that I showed used to take my arm

66

band in his jaws and insist on trotting around the ring with it in his mouth, much to the hilarity of the spectators and the other contestants. Of course many of the judges also thought it was funny, and it would quite naturally focus their attention on my Chesapeake. By the way, he finished his championship quite easily. If you try this but the judge asks you to take the arm band and put it on like everyone else does, do it.

Another important thing: start showing your Chesapeake as soon as you enter the ring. Even though the judge hasn't lined the dogs up, he is still looking and might form an opinion early.

Before going any further, let me describe the classes at the dog show and your dog's progression through them. We will assume that you have entered your pup in the Puppy Class. If your dog receives a blue ribbon (wins the class), you settle down and wait. The next class shown is Novice. After Novice comes the Bred-by-Exhibitor Class. This is open only to dogs that were actually bred by the person who is showing the dog. After this comes the American-bred Class, open only to dogs bred in this country. Then comes the Open Class, open to any Chesapeake. You could have entered your puppy in any of the foregoing classes (except Bred-by-Exhibitor—unless you bred him), but you were smart and entered him in the Puppy Class where he belongs.

When the winner of the Open Class has been determined, then the winners of each class enter the ring for the judge to determine the Winners Dog, Winners Bitch, and Best of Winners. As a general rule, the Best of Winners dog emerges from the Open Class, but a well-trained pup sometimes is selected.

The Winners Dog and Winners Bitch both receive points toward their championship. The judging goes on with both of these competing with any Chessies that have already attained their championship title entering the ring as "Specials." From these dogs, the judge selects the Best of Breed and Best of Opposite Sex.

At an all-breed show, the Chesapeake winning Best of Breed goes on to compete with other Sporting Dogs for Best in Group. Should he win the Group, he goes on to compete for Best in Show.

If your Chessie has won the blue ribbon in the Puppy Class, it will be in the Winners Class (and hopefully in succeeding classes) that all of your work and preparation will stand you in good stead. Never stop showing, even when you are sure the judge is not looking in your direction. You never know when he will turn suddenly. The gaiting is of primary importance with the Chesapeake. Make sure that your Chessie moves smoothly along by your side, always on a loose leash and always under complete control. Take your time about moving and don't let the judge fluster you. Just show your dog. But remember these important points: try to enter the ring first and have your dog set up where the judge designates; move your dog on a loose leash and always keep showing.

Good luck!

Champion Mount Joy's Benjimin, owned by Helen Fleischmann.

Pictured here are scenes from the Lancaster Kennel Club Show, Chesapeake Specialty, 1977. At left, dogs and handlers move to positions in line around the ring.

Right: Dogs and handlers wait for the judge's instructions.

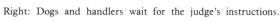

Left: The judge begins his inspection.

Chesapeakes in the Show Ring

Because I told you in the preceding chapter—in great detail—how to show your Chesapeake, I will limit this chapter to shows in general and Chesapeakes in particular.

Until a comparatively short time ago, Chesapeakes were not well regarded as "show" dogs. It was generally assumed that the majority of Chesapeakes were used mainly in field trials and for hunting. The Chesapeake certainly is not as flashy and glamorous as the Golden Retriever, but is rather solid and stolid, and he just seems to lumber along.

Another detraction was the "loading of shoulder" in the Chesapeake, which most judges would penalize, but which actually was a result of hard work and excessive running or even swimming. Now, some show enthusiasts will not agree with me, but believe this because it is true.

The main reason Chesapeakes have started to do a moderate amount of Group placing and even some Group winning is that some "just show" kennels have sprung up and point directly toward show.

Another reason that more Chesapeakes are placing in the Group is the fact that many field trial enthusiasts have made serious efforts to finish their good field trial champions as dual champions. Two from the West Coast are the late Helen Fleischmann of Mount Joy Kennels and Eloise Heller of Baronland Kennels.

In the East the last great field kennel that brought its Chesapeakes into the show ring with great success was August and Louise Belmont's South Bay Kennels. Because my wife and I were intimately associated with this endeavor, I will tell you about it.

The first Chesapeake that my wife (the former Ruth Williams) and I showed for the Belmonts was Amateur Field Champion Bomarc of Southbay. Bo was completely field bred, but he had good comformation, and after he found out what we wanted, he rather enjoyed "hamming it up." The pleasant part of showing the Belmonts' dogs was the fact that it coincided with our "madcap existence" at that time. On Saturday we would take a load of dogs, including Bomarc and several other Retrievers, to a dog show. As soon as the judging was completed, we would make a beeline for New Jersey, Pennsylvania, Long Island, or wherever the field trial was to be held the next day. There Bomarc would be delivered to Augie Belmont, and he would run in the Amateur All-Age Stake.

If we arrived at the show early enough and there was a pond nearby, Bomarc liked nothing better than a good swim a few hours before entering the show ring.

Remember, a Chesapeake's coat dries off in minutes, much faster than that of the other Retriever breeds.

Bomarc finished his championship in the breed ring handily and then was relegated back to the field. If he had been campaigned as heavily as some of the "pure show" specimens around, I am sure he could have made some Group wins.

The next two Chesapeakes that we introduced to the show ring for the Belmonts were South Bay Nike and Cherokee's South Bay Project.

Nike was an excellent bitch. Although she never finished either on the bench or in the field, she made her mark in both. Nike was Winners Bitch at one Chesapeake Specialty Show and Best of Winners at another. She acquired a respectable number of points in Derby Stakes and placed in at least one Qualifying Stake before an unfortunate operation ended both her bench and her field careers.

Although South Bay Nike presumably was undetectable from other Chesapeakes in the show ring, judges invariably would ask me how she was doing in the field. Something just stamps the field dogs.

Cherokee's South Bay Project, known generally and affectionately as "Larry," was a great show dog, but he thought the whole thing was rather amusing. Before he was introduced to the show ring, Larry had amassed thirty-two points in Derby Stakes, thus ranking fourth in the country in 1964 for all Retriever breeds, and at this writing fourth for all time in Derby points for Chesapeakes.

Larry took the show ring by storm. He lost very few times, and often in winning he went Best of Breed over long-time Chesapeake bench champions that were heavily campaigned.

My wife and I had the pleasure of owning Larry for the last eleven years of his life, and he certainly was a joy to have around. He was our personal shooting dog for almost all of that time but never was entered in another field trial or shown in the breed ring. I think, all in all, he was happier bringing in an occasional big fat goose for our table.

There is no doubt in my mind but that the Chesapeake fancy suffered a heavy blow when the Belmonts switched to Labradors for the field. Winning, though, is the name of the game. That's what the trials are all about. I was welcomed with open arms when I first handled my Retrievers at trials—as long as they weren't especially good, or stayed in Derby. But when they started to press in Open, forget it. The same holds true for the breed ring game, only more so.

Looking back to the time when Chesapeakes were first beginning to be shown in the conformation ring, we find that Jupiter, Floss, and Browney IV were the first three Chesapeakes to finish in the breed ring, finishing

Chesapeake Specialty, 1977. Lining up for the judge's inspection.

during 1910, 1911, and 1912, respectively. One of the earliest winning kennels and one that is still showing and winning is Chesacroft Kennels. Chesacroft Tobe, Chesacroft Drake, and Chesacroft Queen all finished their bench championships during 1922 and 1923. Chesacroft continued their winning ways, finishing four more Chesapeakes in 1925, 1926, and 1927.

In 1931, Anthony Bliss finished his first Chesapeake on the bench—Busy B—and I will wager that he also ran in trials. In 1933 Mr. Bliss also finished Bud Parker's Ripple, a Chesapeake that I distinctly remember in trials. In fact, there was more than a smattering of straight field bred dogs competing successfully in the show ring up to the time Mrs. Daniel Horn finished her first Chesapeake with her kennel name of Eastern Waters. This was Tempest of Eastern Waters.

Eastern Waters, I believe, was the first strictly show and obedience kennel of Chesapeakes that made its mark. That is, unless you were to consider Chesacroft a show kennel—which it is not.

There are only six dual champion Chesapeakes at this writing, and I think their names bear repeating (without

Chesapeake Specialty, 1977. Preparing for the judge's inspection.

all of the titles, though). The first was Sodak's Gypsy Prince, owned by Chesacroft Kennels. See, I told you Chesacroft isn't strictly a show kennel. Then came Mount Joy's Mallard, owned by E. C. Fleischmann, in 1959. Eloise Heller had two dual champions, Baron's Tule Tiger, in 1965, and Tiger's Cub, in 1970. In between, Dr. Dashnaw finished Meg's O'Timothey both in the field and on the bench. And also in 1970, the late Mike Paterno did the same with Koolwater Colt of Tritown.

I am not going to bore you by listing all of the bench champions the Chesapeake breed has created. A complete list is available, at least through 1975, in the

Champion Kepple's Atom Toko, owned by Katherine A. Kepple and handled by Cleo Friedericksen.

most recent Chesapeake Year Book. I will, however, bring you up to date by listing the Chesapeakes that were recorded as bench champions in *The American Kennel Gazette* from January 1976 through December 1980.

If you study these listings you will see who the multi-registrees are. In other words, which owners or kennels have been most active in the show ring during the past few years.

Note that (D) after the name denotes *Dog* and (B) *Bitch*. Other abbreviations that appear in these listings are: C.D., Companion Dog; C.D.X., Companion Dog Excellent; and T.D., Tracking Dog. The significance of these titles is explained in the chapter on the Chesapeake in obedience.

BENCH CHAMPIONS—JANUARY 1976
THROUGH DECEMBER 1980

Dog	Owner
Bold Regard of Green Acre (D)	Frank Garcia
Coco of Stebbins Brook, C.D. (B)	Beverly E. Roach
Marpa's Rip of Chesapine (D)	Mr. & Mrs. P. Clark
Amigo's Charlie of Costa Mesa (D)	L. Arnold & L. A. Smith
Briarmoor's Spatterdock (D)	Bruce Leakey
Cascades Cinder (B)	Carolyn A. Sears
Chesachobee's Bold Baron, C.D. (D)	M. Tellander & M. Buchholz
Chesaford's Oak n'Honey (B)	Mr. & Mrs. Charles Cranford
Timothy Joe (D)	D. & R. Lunsford
Charlies Tootsie Pop (B)	Mary E. Laughton
Chesrite's Misty Harbor, C.D. (B)	Jan M. & Jody M. Thomas
Wildwood's Prince Baranoff, C.D. (D)	C. A. Sears & L. P. Harger
Twin Rivers Ivan (D)	S. P. & B. G. Adams
Berteleda Santana (D)	Richard Allen & Carole Clement
Cub's Blasted Goose (B)	Stephanie P. & David W. Beach
Funky Brownie of Rapids (B)	Margarethe A. & Bruce Bjelland
Hi-Ho's Orange Blossom Special (B)	Stephen E. & Ellen Loftsgaard
Kasties Christie of Snocre (B)	John E. Schmidt
Nicolay's River Queen (B)	Charles Nicolay
Snocre's Wild Rover (D)	John E. Schmidt
Silhouette's Echo (B)	Ortance H. Swanson
Captain Buffy (D)	Maxene H. Elmore
Eastern Waters Chese V Zybura (B)	Jere Zybura
Marpa's Captain Kidd (D)	Mr. & Mrs. Paul W. Clark
Teals Tiger (D)	Susan Hatfield
Twin River's Jinger (B)	Frank & Cookie Evangelho
Briarmoors Bear Paw (D)	Patricia Leakey
Chesachobee's Mary Rider (B)	Mildred G. Buckley
Eastern Waters' Thundercloud (D)	Val Cartwright & Fran Spangle
Smokey Glenne Chesa BB (B)	Mildred Buchholz
Chesapine's Frosty Morn (B)	R. W. & L. M. Berg
Cogley's P R Going Chessie (B)	Fred K. & Rosemary Hahn
Crosswinds Flying Gee Bee (B)	Mr. & Mrs. Kent D. Lowman
Donwens American Horse (D)	Maxine Gurin
Nanticoke Sir Woodrow Drake (D)	Robert L. Baker, Jr.
Briarmoors Dynamite (D)	Patricia & Bruce Leakey
Cogley's Penny Ante (B)	L. D. & S. M. Cogley
Eastern Waters' Ever Amber, T.D. (B)	Susan Horn
Kalin's Anniversary (B)	Kayo Moss
Kalua Bear of Crazy Camp (B)	Pam Lloyd
The Centurian (D)	Wm. J. Stunkel
Canadien Club of Wyndam (D)	Edward J. Atkins
Cub's Chesareid Fireball (B)	Dr. Marston & Judith Ann Jones
Titan's Orion (D)	Mary E. Laughton
Chesaford Yankee Phoebe (B)	David & Janice Rosenbaum
Misty's Rusty McGee (D)	L. Arnold & Leigh A. Smith
Mitsu Kuma's Rum Bun (B)	Barbara L. & Samuel H. Mullen III
Skipper XII (D)	Adey May Dunnell
Baron's Sandy Boy (B)	D. J. & K. E. Miller
Bay Barron (D)	John D. Hahn
Mount Joy's Bellflower, C.D. (B)	Frances Anderson
Cogley's P R Yahoo Sicum (D)	Suzanne M. Cogley
Cubs Wet Water Willie (D)	Tom D. Burns
Chesareid Precious Gem, C.D. (B)	Scott Ansley & Sybil Reid
Eastern Waters' Chieftain, C.D. (D)	Marguerite Willis
Jane's Ruby Anne (B)	C. E. & F. J. LeRoy
Snocre's Sportin' Life (B)	John E. Schmidt
Blustrywood Great Lakes Gal (B)	Kyle C. James
Cascade's Razzle Dazzle (B)	C. A. & R. J. Sears
Eastern Waters Cimarron (B)	J. P. Horn & E. H. Humer
Gaymerry Something Else (B)	Elizabeth Grogran
Snocre's On The Spot (D)	Barbara & Katherine Scherrer

Champion Chesrite's Justin Tyme, C.D., going Best of Breed under judge Lyle Ring. His second Specialty win, this was Justin's fifty-ninth consecutive Best of Breed win, and he had just completed the second leg toward his C.D.X. and was highest scoring Champion of Record in Trial. Justin was always breeder-owner handled by Jan Thomas and Jody Thomas.

Canadian Champion Chesrite's Harbor Master going Best of Winners. With this win "Ben" finished his American championship with four consecutive majors. Owned by Martha C. Thorne and Jan Thomas, Ben was handled to his American championship by the latter.

Above: The Futurity winner at the Lancaster Kennel Club Show, Chesapeake Specialty, 1977.

Below: The Chesapeake is trained to "Stay."

Below: Sire and dam of the Winners Dog, these two Chesapeakes were Best of Breed and Best of Opposite Sex at the 1977 Lancaster Kennel Club Show.

Dog	Owner
Tricrowns Kimbinga (D)	Erica Woodman
Eastern Waters' Statesman (D)	Joyce Lucarelli
Joshua of Burning Tree (D)	M. A. & J. M. Lindquist
My Gal Sal of Kalifonski (B)	Lottie Edelman
Oak n' Thistle's Captain (D)	Caroline R. Stewart
Shore Waters Michigan (D)	Margaretta S. Fisher
Woodrivers Shea of Chesapine (D)	R. W. & L. M. Berg
Bever's Misty Reef (D)	R. M. & C. E. Kelly
Blustrywoods Chapel Sunday (B)	Karen A. & John W. Wood, Jr.
Chesrite's Harbor Master (D)	Martha Thorne & Jan Thomas
Chevron's Mighty Riley (D)	Emmett S. Heinrich
Frosty Bobs Duke of Targele (D)	Renn & Cynthia Luebber
Kaste's Cleo of Snocre (B)	John E. Schmidt
Berteleda Binavere, C.D. (B)	Nancy D. & Leslie A. Lowenthal
Chesachobee's Golden Sand, C.D., T.D. (B)	M. G. Buccholz & Scott Jones
Crosswinds Flying Rocket (B)	Brenda Joan Lawry
Hi-Ho's Cutthroat (D)	Douglas Price Hanson
Kep-Ple's Atom Toko (D)	Katherine A. Kepple
Magic Waters' Tally Cindy (B)	Bruce & Val Cartwright
Z-Bets Bay Galaxie (B)	Juanita L. Weaver
Chesachobee's Ruf N Redi, C.D. (D)	Sharon Young
Eastern Waters' Lightning (D)	Valerie A. & Bruce L. Cartwright
Jonathan Livingston Seagull (D)	Susan & Jack P. Hatfield
Blustrywoods Big Buck (D)	Kyle C. James & Anita L. James; John W. Wood, Jr. & K. Wood
Briarmoor's Windflower (B)	Patricia A. & Nancy P. Leakey
Butch Duckmaster Cameron (D)	Rick K. & Janet M. Cameron
Chess-Acre Sandy (B)	Eugene F. Hobart
Chesterfield of Chelsea (D)	Charles H. Livengood, Jr.
Eastern Waters' Revere (D)	Mr. & Mrs. Paul Clark
Evansland Firecracker Belle, C.D. (B)	Steven D. Iverson & Gayl & Donald D. Iverson
Kobi's California Quail, C.D. (D)	John A. Smart & Frank Garrett
Marpa's Kit Kimberly (B)	Mr. & Mrs. Paul W. Clark
Wayward's Chociat Splash (B)	John B. & Mary Welles, Ramsey & Clyde Wilkerson
Chesachobee's Ovedio Muue, C.D. (B)	Dianna D. Blakey
Chesafords Chestnut Newfy (D)	Mr. & Mrs. Ch. E. Cranford
Eastern Waters Chesaford Sun (D)	Mr. & Mrs. Ch. E. Cranford
J & J's Maudie of Highview (B)	Jacob Gatrell
Jerry's Drake of Chesiecan (D)	Jerry & Cathy Graham
Sandy of Klamath (B)	James W. & Theora F. Copeland
Snocre's Kiss Me Kate (B)	Ellen J. Madans & John E. Schmidt
Sunwig Farm Teal (D)	Benda J. & David H. Lawry
Blustrywoods Chapel Bell (B)	Karen Ann & John W. Wood, Jr.
Suzie-Q (B)	Robert L. Lunsford & Susan Hatfield
Z's Danny Canuck, C.D. (D)	Arthur & Mary E. Mazzola
Briarmoors' Water Chief (D)	John H. Cargol
Cascade Tahoe Tallac (D)	Peggy Ann Dunne & Carolyn A. Sears
Chesaford's Toy Trucker (D)	Charles E. Cranford
Cogleys Benjamin Franklin (D)	Rick Neumann
Crosswinds Flying Red Devil (B)	Mr. & Mrs. K. Lowman
Eastern Waters Charg'n Knight (D)	Nathaniel Horn
Misty Morn's Cinnamon Cinder, C.D. (B)	Julia A. & Lorne Cole
Northcreek Tule Tunk (D)	Maggie D. Hoagland
Snocre's Excess Baggage (B)	Eileen J. Schmidt
Teds Great Northern Spike (D)	Paul E. Pinnow
Burt's Bama Cocoa Bear (D)	Alburta D. Lowe
Chesapine's Tula (B)	Lorraine M. & Raymond W. Berg
Chesavieda's Ornamental Buoy, C.D.X., T.D. (D)	Dianna D. Blakey
Donwens Daisy of Poisett (B)	George & Pauline E. Henshaw
Kiska of Noyes Island (B)	Samuel Ralph Rocci
Snocre's in the Spirit (B)	Barbara J. Scherrer & John E. Schmidt

Dog	Owner
Stormy of Shilo (B)	Sherry Lee Massey
Cassiphone of Pondview (B)	Christine Eller
Chesareid Sandys Brandy (B)	L. Arnold & Leigh A. Smith
Chestnut Hills Penny (B)	Karen W. Anderson
Eastern Waters Zachariah (D)	Kenneth & Diane Lutters
Admiral Jonathan Peake (D)	Herbert & Hazel Halper
Blustrywood Dynamite Carlo (D)	Karen Ann Wood
Cesarab's Daddy's Girl (B)	Valerie Cartwright & Sheila DiVaccaro
Hi-Ho Ironeyes Cody O'Snocre (D)	Stephen & Ellen Loftsgaard
Ali's Neptune Jesseka (B)	Eileen M. Antolino
Crosswinds Flying Ranger (B)	Roger Coelho & Barbara Ann Coelho
Lazy H's King of Cub (D)	Lloyd & Nancy Hermes
Monkton Yankee Clipper, C.D. (D)	Thomas T. & Patricia A. Stohler
Pattie's Tricia (B)	Wm. P. Ranftl
Springflow Fandango (B)	Joyce L. Lucarelli
Allen's Pond Gooseberry (D)	Richard & Dorothy C. Wertz
Gung Ho Leal (B)	Adey May Dunnell
Snocre's Curly Bead (D)	Jamie Arnold
Appollo's Cogley Racin Jason (D)	Fred K. & Rosemarie A. Hahn
Blustrywood's Brandywein (B)	Kenneth W. Sparks
Jaia's Beau of Barkley (D)	Kyle C. & Anita James & Karen Ann & John W. Wood, Jr.
Josie Lee of Little River Farm, C.D. (B)	Jane Kelso Ballou
Shari's Teddy Bear (B)	Sharon Gannaway
Chugar of Coca Bear, C.W.D. (D)	Clarence W. Daugette III
Skipper's Big John (D)	Adey May Dunnell
Windown Bull of Bull Hill (D)	Scott W. & Suzanne Skinner
Chesapine's Audacious Coffee (B)	Raymond & Lorraine M. Berg
Eastern Waters Betsy Ross, C.D.X. (B)	E. Christopher & Susan Cone
Eastern Waters Chesaford Rus (B)	Mr. & Mrs. Charles Cranford
Kep-Pies Cherokee Sal (B)	Katherine A. Kepple
Longcove's Spring Serenade (B)	Kathie A. & Jeanne K. Kinney
Marpa's Kidd Kado (D)	Gary J. & Judi Abegglen
Mitso Kuma's Robbin (B)	Bill Smith
Shady's Abraham (D)	Nancy McGauley
Skipper's Big John (D)	Adey M. Dunnell
Spirit of Alnwick Castle (B)	Susan L. Lamielle & Michael Lamielle
Chesapine's Misty Autumn Oak (D)	Kurt E. & Patricia J. Wagner
Crosswinds Flying Voodoo (B)	Diane B. Hankin
Muff's Steel Shot Hunter Boy (D)	Bill Smith
Rook's Blasting Cap (B)	James Ray
Snocre's Bing (D)	John E. Schmidt & Bruce D. Baker
Eastern Waters Yankee, C.D. (D)	Rupert J. & Eliz. H. Humer
Hi-Ho's Anglo Spice (B)	Stephen & Ellen Loftsgaard
Hi-Ho's Dear Abbey of Snocre (B)	John E. & Ellen J. Schmidt
Briarmoor's Leaping Trout (B)	Victoria A. Downham
Mitsu Kuma's Saxon Pond (D)	Wm. C. & Dyane M. Baldwin
Snocre's Daisy Clover (B)	Carolyn McLoughlin & John E. Schmidt
Rockrun's Swift Water (B)	Diane Hankin
Chesrite Littlrivr Nightyme, C.D. (D)	Jan M. Thomas
FC Cub's Kobi King (D)	Charles P. Sambrailo, Sr.
Redlon's J. J. Sample (D)	Mary Jane Pappler
Shiloh's Stormy Sunday (D)	Guy & Agnes Grieve
Willowpond Water off a Duxbak (D)	Douglas P. & Edith T. Hanson
Briarwoods Holy Moses (D)	William Ranftl
Eastern Waters Black Pt Leo, C.D. (D)	Elizabeth H. Humer
Eastern Waters' Coeur De Lion (D)	J. P. & Dr. Daniel Horn
High Plains Ruff-N-Ready, C.D. (D)	Betty J. Smith
Ironstone's Hot Chocolate (D)	Yasemin Demirtas
Jessica Lamb, C.D. (B)	Tobi Rae Carnine
Luke's Maggie (B)	Joyce L. Lucarelli
Rocky Bays Canadien Mist (B)	Roberta A. Johnson
Shore Waters Jiminy Cricket (B)	Julie A. Norton

Above: Setting the dogs up for the judge's inspection.

Below: The judge makes his inspection.

Below: Two handlers smile with pleasure as they receive awards at the 1977 Lancaster Kennel Club Show.

73

Above: Handlers and dogs move out at a faster pace.

Above: Handlers and dogs await the judge's approach.

Above: The judge goes to the end of the line as he makes his inspection of the dogs.

Dog	Owner
Cocoa Princess Ann (B)	Robert Albaugh
Gringo II (D)	Lloyd D. & Suzanne M. Cogley
Lisa's Tonka (B)	Roman W. & Jeanne L. Schwartz
Chesachobee's Chesavieda (B)	Dianna D. Blakey
Chesachobee's Naya's Nina (B)	Nancy S. Naya
Chesachobee's White Wave (B)	Harry Weiskittel, Jr. & Mildred Buchholz
Chesareid Easter Token (D)	Sybil Reid
Eastern Waters Damariscotta (B)	Janet P. Horn & Ranee Nevels
Hi-Ho's Hamm's Bear (D)	James E. Kite
Snocre's Little Pistol (B)	Deborah A. & Charles Brewer
Wynhams Algonquin (D)	Mr. & Mrs. Gerald Szostak & Edward J. Atkins
Snocre's Regal Rusty Nail, C.D. (B)	Lorne M. & Julia A. Cole
Apache's Tequila Suprise (D)	L. Arnold & Leigh A. Smith
Chestnut Hills Tiger (D)	Ronald B. Anderson
Irish's Shining Princess (B)	Gary D. Irish
Kep-Ples Gretchen (B)	Katherine A. Kepple
Muff's Misty Red Robbin Girl (B)	Bill Smith
All American Creme De Cocoa (B)	Michael M. & Rose C. Tucker
All American Tule Buster (D)	Fred Ichelson
Cub's Sonoma Mountain Jack (D)	Victor M. Reid III & Barbara T. Reid
Hi-Ho's Mudslide Slim (D)	Edward & Sharon Bruno
Jala's Fox of Barkley Lake (D)	Kyle C. James & Paul W. Seagers, Jr.
Cotac Heset's Boroimhe (D)	Mary Ann Grafton Rogers
Cur-sans Cinder of Marpa (B)	Sandra D. Dollar
Duke of Dunkirk (D)	Veronica Brooks
Windown Aelwif of Wyndam (B)	Edward J. Atkins
Orion's King Tithonus (D)	Mary E. Laughton & Barbara S. Weddell
Teals Tule Madam, C.D. (B)	Robert L. & Robbin Phillipps
Val-Lee's Sand Pebbles (B)	Sandi Powley
Bert II (D)	Donald Shannon
Berteleda Purdy Game Girl (B)	Nancy D. & Leslie A. Lowenthal
Cubs Shogun of Juanita Bay (D)	Tom D. Ivey, M.D.
Hi-Ho's Rocky Mountain High (D)	Charles A. Burke
Northwind Dales Mocha (B)	Dale L. Weese
Snocre's Hi-Ho's Timia Lass (B)	Thresesa Petray
John Shamus (D)	Adey M. Dunnell
Kojak Toko's Spittin' Image (D)	Katherine A. Kepple
Miss Muffitt (B)	Adey M. Dunnell
Silhouette's Jake (D)	Ortance H. Swanson
Sue-Tim's Reflection (D)	Tracy Young
Cub's Cinnamon Chieftain (D)	Steven P. Harmon
Heir of Alnwick Castle, C.D. (D)	Michael & Susan Lamielle
Tallizar Sayzar, C.D. (B)	Mary Teresa Brown
Woodhelven's Brother Bark (D)	Michael J. Baumgartner
Woodhelven's Golden Pride (B)	Ann & Michael Baumgartner
Chesachobee's Rusty Red (D)	Angel E. & Nancy Naya
Little River Annie Come Lately (B)	Kenneth F. & Linda Higgins

Handler and dog respond to the judge's instructions.

Handler and dog move rapidly as the judge watches.

Dog	Owner
Polo's Sande Dandee (D)	Eddie L. & Doris Manker
Poolside's Larena of Shiloh (B)	Susan L. & Michael Lamielle
Sandy Oak's Sam Hill, C.D. (D)	David J. & Kathleen E. Miller
Snocre's Major Gun (D)	John E. & Ellen J. Schmidt
Willowpond Mandarin Duck (B)	Mark Tichenor & Edith Hanson
Willowpond Sitting Duck (D)	Jill & Robert S. Latchaw
Sir Basil Curry (D)	Frederick T. Dombo, Jr.
Snocre's Upsa Daisy (B)	Douglas R. & Salley E. Mayfield
Chestnut Hill's Coke, C.D.X. (B)	Karen W. Anderson
Jala's Herbert Happy Hunter (D)	Donald J. Meldrum & Kyle C. James
Limefield Magnolia (B)	Marie Whitney Bonadies
Chodam's Apache Star, C.D. (B)	Micky Tellander
Hi-Ho Gunner's Bang (B)	Ellen Loftsgaard & Theresa Petray
Baron's Brown Bear II (D)	Mike Carrithers
Chesapine's Surf and Turf (D)	Lorraine & Raymond W. Berg
Chestnut Hills Bruiser, C.D., T.D. (D)	Ronald B. Anderson
Mitsu Kuma's Captain Nemo (D)	Sandra S. Nichols
Quellwater Unce The Bear (D)	Ilse Fass
Slingshot's Boomerang, U.D.T. (B)	B. W. & Beverly A. Hirsig
Snap's Crackle (B)	Charlene R. Coleman
Foxridge's Pat C. Cinnamon (B)	Shirli J. Hayes
Magnum Force of Darkwood (D)	Paul D. & Jackie A. Shidla
Neptune's Darkstar Diana (B)	Eileen M. Antolino
Terra's Chocolate Lady (B)	Shirli J. Hayes
Z's Arrows Brown Brigette (B)	Donald R. Cornelius & Mary Ellen Mazzola
Z's Morgandy Teak (D)	Janis Ann Tobey
Chesavieda's Sedge Mouse, C.D. (B)	Gale S. Von Herbulis & Dianna D. & Jeffrey H. Blakey
Crosswinds Flying X-Ray (D)	Julia V. Palmer
Miss Dawn of Ferdinand, C.D. (B)	Kathy Graham
Poisett's Dark Molasses (B)	George & Pauline E. Henshaw
Rockrun's Chippewa Tule (B)	Diane B. Hankin
Rockrun's Penny Popcorn (B)	Diane B. Hankin
Chesrite's One More Tyme (B)	Jan M. Thomas
Darclans Ginger of October (B)	Bev A. & Tom Mindykowski
Grit's Oak 'N Thistle Ember (B)	Dr. J. & B. Stewart & Dr. Timothy J. Carrion
Hi-Ho's Calcutta of Snocree (B)	Stephen & Ellen Loftsgaard
Neptune's King of Campgaw (D)	Michael R. Antolino, Sr.
Poisett's Benjamin Too (D)	George & Pauline E. Henshaw
Aleutian Sand, C.D. (D)	William J. & Victoria S. Fenili
Buffy Star-Gazer, C.D. (B)	Freddie L. & Francine A. Sichting
Chesachobee's Tachwagh (D)	Jackie & Duane Drummond
Donwen's Chesica Joy, C.D. (B)	Gail Putnam
Longcove's Chipper (D)	Maurice J. Randall
Shilo's Sasquatch (D)	Verley R. Jones
Toko's Gingersnap (B)	Robert J. Carney

Above: With head up and tail up in proper form, the Chesapeake goes around the ring at a rapid pace.

Above: Handlers and dogs continue around the ring at a fast pace.

Above: A long wait sometimes results in a dog's breaking stance.

Above: A handler repositions her dog's feet.

Above: Handlers make a last-minute check of their dogs.

75

Eastern Waters Betsy Ross, C.D.X., shows that the broad jump is no problem. Breeder, Janet Horn. Owners, Susan and Kit Cone.

The Chesapeake in Obedience Competition

The American Kennel Club approved organized obedience competition and assumed jurisdiction over obedience rules in 1935. Since then, interest has increased at a phenomenal rate, for obedience competition is not only a sport the average spectator can follow readily, but also a sport for which the average owner can train his own dog easily.

The Chesapeake Bay Retriever is well known in obedience competition and ranks high as compared with all other breeds. Many owners who are field trial enthusiasts take their Chesapeakes through the training and the competition for the Companion Dog (C.D.) title, for basic obedience training is a must in field trial training.

For five of the six obedience titles, competition differs from bench show and field trial competition in that dogs do not compete against each other but are judged on their response to certain commands. Thus there is no limit to the number of dogs that may win in such competition, for each dog is scored individually on the basis of a point rating system.

Three of the titles are progressive: "C.D."—Companion Dog; "C.D.X."—Companion Dog Excellent and "U.D."—Utility Dog. Because they are progressive, earlier titles are dropped as a dog acquires the next higher title. For each of these three titles the dog must gain a score of at least 170 points out of a possible total of 200 in three successive trials under different judges. No score in any one exercise may be less than 50 percent of the points allotted.

A fourth title, the "T.D." or Tracking Dog title, may be won at any time and tests for it are held apart from dog shows. The owner of a dog that holds both a U.D. and a T.D. may use the letters "U.D.T." after the name of the dog, signifying Utility Dog Tracker.

Effective July 1, 1977, The American Kennel Club approved the awarding of the title "O.T. Ch."—Obedience Trial Champion. To be eligible for this title, a dog must have earned the Utility Dog title and then must earn one hundred points in certain types of competition, placing first three times under different judges. It is for this title, of course, that dogs compete against each other.

In late 1979, the Board of Directors of The American Kennel Club approved the test for the "T.D.X." title, to become effective March 1, 1980. Eligibility to compete for this title is limited to dogs that have already earned the Tracking Dog title.

CalBak Saba'ka's Babe, C.D., owned by Marion G. Bleser.

Trials for obedience trained dogs are held at most of the larger bench shows, and obedience training clubs are to be found in almost all communities today. Information concerning forthcoming trials and lists of obedience training clubs are included regularly in *Pure Bred Dogs—American Kennel Gazette* and other magazines. Pamphlets containing rules and regulations governing obedience competition are available upon request from The American Kennel Club, 51 Madison Avenue, New York, NY 10010. Rules are revised occasionally, so if you are interested in participating in obedience competition, you should be sure your copy of the regulations is current.

Most of the field trial people and also the show people are well aware of the astuteness of the Chesapeake in obedience, and many of them take full advantage of it. As you read this book, you will note that many Chesapeakes that are either bench or field trial champions also have earned one or more degrees in obedience. With the Chesapeake, proficiency in obedience seems to come naturally.

Recently I wrote to Eloise Heller Cherry to ask about the Chesapeake's place as a Seeing Eye Dog, for Mrs. Cherry is a leader in this field. She replied that the Chesapeake's service as a Seeing Eye Dog had been discontinued some ten or eleven years ago because Chesapeakes are too possessive with their masters. This is regrettable, but it is very true that Chesapeakes are very possessive.

On the pages that follow are listings of Chesapeakes which have earned obedience titles recorded in *The American Kennel Gazette* from January 1976 through December 1980.

As in other listings, (D) following a dog's name signifies *Dog*, and (B), *Bitch*. "Ch." preceding a dog's name indicates that he has earned a championship in bench shows.

Eastern Waters Betsy Ross, C.D.X., executes the "Retrieve over High Jump."

OBEDIENCE TITLES—JANUARY 1976 THROUGH DECEMBER 1980

Dog	*Owner*
Companion Dogs—1976	
Chesachobee's Ovedio Mille (B)	Dianna D. Blakey
Ch. Chesachobee's Pandora (B)	Mildred Buchholz
Eastern Waters' Cloudcraft (B)	Robert & Linda Lubitz
Ch. Chesachobee's Bronze Atlas (D)	Mildred Buchholz
Evansland Firecracker Belle (D)	Steven D. Iverson & Gayle & Donald Iverson
Mount Joy's E. C. Bay (D)	F. G. & Janis Nicholas
Portlands Hustler (B)	Jon B. Perry
Magellan's Dutchman, T.D. (D)	E. J. Frinkman
Temple's Ginger Bay (B)	J. D. & S. E. Mathis, Jr.
Wildwood's Prince Baranof (D)	Carolyn A. Sears & Linda P. Harger
Chesachobee's Fantastic (B)	Mr. & Mrs. Ch. E. Cranford
Eastern Waters' Betsy Ross (B)	C. & S. Cone
Major Bruno of Sandy Hook (D)	Isabel & Laura Griffith
Odin's Chester (D)	Roger & Barbara Coelho
Ch. Hi-Ho's Aguereberry (D)	E. W. & H. E. Hallett & Ellen Loftsgaard
Salt Pond's Yukon of Alaska (D)	B. L. & D. M. Krischuk
Snocre's Celebate Summer (B)	Ellen Madans & Ben Crowell
Chesachobee's Ruf 'n' Redi (D)	Sharon Young
Chestnut Hill's Dusty (B)	Karen W. Anderson
Eastern Waters' Lady Magellan (B)	Kay Hale
Gyp's Sassy Bay (B)	Ora Meyer
Bender's Pride Megan (B)	Jos. F. Benefides, Jr.
Eastern Waters' Chieftain (D)	Marguerite Willis
Breakwater's Flagon Dragon (D)	Ch. L. & Elizabeth H. Morris
Crosswind's Flying Orion (D)	Eunice Wynne & W. O. Stoke, Jr.
J. A. Kelly's Clancy (D)	Mrs. Judith Kelly
Eastern Waters' Little Acooma (B)	Henry J. Kudlinski
Eastern Waters' Thundercloud (D)	Val Cartwright & Fran Spangle
Jennifer's Joe of Wye Lake (D)	Donald C. Walsh
Red's Ginger Lodge (B)	Jeff Little
Bronze Bay at Sunset (D)	Tawni Lyn Crippen
Cogley's P R Betsy Ross (B)	Bill Coryell
Ch. Eastern Waters' Chese V Zybura (B)	Jere Zybura
Josie Lee of Little River Farm (B)	Jane K. Fraser
Ch. Kaste's Christie of Snocre (B)	John E. Schmidt
Companion Dogs Excellent—1976	
Cub's Minnesota Patsy (B)	Donald D. Gayle & Steven Iverson
Koolwater's Little Beaver (B)	G. Norman Herberg
Ch. Chesachobee's Bold Baron (D)	Mickey Tellander & Mildred Buchholz
Mount Joy's Winkle (D)	
Berteleda Kobi (B)	Carl M. Larkin & Alice J. Lyon
Tess (B)	David Warren & Stephanie P. Beach
Ch. Chesachobee's Papoose (B)	Marguerite D. Willis
Utility Dogs—1976	
Chesachobee's Cocoanut, T.D. (B)	Dianna D. & B. R. Blakey
Companion Dogs—1977	
Crosswinds Flying Kamvair (D)	Karen Schoenben
Eastern Waters' Takanossee (B)	Susan Horn & Eliz. H. Humer
Topsy of Dayton (B)	Kristen & Frank Garrett
Briarmoor's Sun Hawk (B)	K. M. & R. C. Taylor
Cub's Taysa (B)	C. P. & J. Lilly
First Cabin Duke (D)	Ralph E. Turner
T's Heller (B)	John Keroak
Z's Danny Canuck (D)	A. & M. E. Mazzola
Chesareida's Ornamental Buoy (D)	Dianna Blakey
Eastern Waters Yankee (D)	Rupert J. & Elizabeth H. Humer
Ima Sandy Too (D)	David J. & Kathleen E. Miller
Berteleda Binavere (B)	Nancy D. & Leslie A. Lowenthal
Ch. Chesachobee's Gemson (D)	Mildred G. Buchholz
Deschane's Chocolate Delight (B)	James G. & Leigh C. Deschane
Eastern Waters Harvest Gal (B)	S. Jean Simpson

Dog	Owner
Snocre's Sophie Tucker (B)	John E. Schmidt
Ch. Baron's Sandy Bay (B)	David J. & Kathleen E. Miller
Neshiminy Creek Petunia (B)	Mary Jane Pappler
Z's Holly Echo (B)	John J. & Laura S. McAulay
Tallizar Sayzar (B)	Mary Teresa Brown
Triumphant Azure Dee (B)	Erin P. Davidson
Ch. Beaver's Misty Reef (D)	Robert M. & Cary E. Kelly
Cherokee Blue Chip (D)	James C. Deschane
Chessie of Barkley Lake (B)	Richard N. Laplant
Duke of Garth (D)	Dominic A. & Diane B. Pelino
Frisco Valley Rain Drop (B)	Rosemary Parsons
Kobl's California Quail (D)	John A. Smart & Frank Barrett

Companion Dogs Excellent—1977

Dog	Owner
Chesachobee's Ovideo Millie (B)	Dianna D. Blakey
Evansland Firecracker Belle (B)	Steven D. & Gayle & Donald Iverson
Magellan's Dutchman, T.D. (D)	E. J. Frinkman
Ch. Crosswinds Flying Explorer (D)	Herbert L. Swinney & D. A. Culp
Ch. Chesareid Precious Gem (B)	Scott Ansley & Sybil Reid
Ch. Eastern Waters Chese V Zybura (B)	Jere Zybura
Shari's Baron of Grey Cloud (D)	Mrs. Patricia Gannaway

Companion Dogs—1978

Dog	Owner
Kara Allan (B)	Sherri & Dano Derr
Montauk Waters Genie (B)	Jennifer L. Cone
Chesachobee's Donner, T.D. (D)	Carole Borthwick
Ch. Cub's Lady Belle (B)	Mrs. Ronald Anderson
Ch. Eastern Waters Chesaford Sun (D)	Mr. & Mrs. Ch. E. Cranford
Cub's Bloody Red Baron (D)	Dean A. & Sally Diess
Eastern Waters Mitsu Kuma Cub (B)	Sharron L. Mullen
Monkton Yankee Clipper (D)	Thomas T. & Patricia A. Stohler
Cogley's Klamath Sacajawea (B)	Lois R. Coryell
L J's Prince O Ke Lani Kal (D)	Lyle J. & Donna B. Ulrich
Ch. Shore Waters Michigan (D)	Margarita S. Fisher
Slingshot's Boomerang (B)	B. W. & Beverley A. Hirsig
Summer Woods Topaz (B)	Brad Hodges
Spin of Cattail Creek (B)	Alice R. Schumacher
Ch. Cascades Razzle Dazzle (B)	Carolyn A. & Ronald J. Sears
Ch. Chesaford's Oak N' Honey (B)	Mr. & Mrs. Ch. E. Cranford
JayEls Jessie Crosswinds (B)	Holly J. Swanson
Miss Dawn of Ferdinand (B)	Kathy Graham
Sandy Oak's Jessyca (B)	Barbara T. & Victor M. Reid III
Dale's Ginger Snap (B)	Robert L. Scattini
De Nemours Gem of Birkenhead (B)	W. D. Mathewson Virginia S. Bixler
Sailor of Foxridge (D)	William H. & Norma D. Vennard
Highplains Ruff-N-Ready (D)	Betty J. Smith
Newrys Duffy (D)	Mariangeles C. Murphy
Bill's Classic Gem (B)	William C. Skobjak
Ch. Browndog Drummond (D)	David Reaves
Ch. Eastern Waters Statesman (D)	Joyce Lucarelli
Ch. Jerry's Drake of Chesiecan (D)	Jerry & Cathy Graham
Thunderwing Acorn (D)	Raymond Muth
Wildwoods Son of a Gun (D)	Kathy Johnson & Susann Martiniuk
Ch. Mitsu Kuma's Rum Bun (B)	Dyane M. Baldwin & Barbara L. Mullen
Mitsu Kuma's Saxon Pond (D)	William C. & Dyane M. Baldwin
Timber's Shadow (D)	Curtis D. Dollar, Jr.
Donwens Maine Guide Stoney (D)	Arlene S. Smith
Snocre's Regal Rusty Nail (B)	Lorne M. & Julia A. Cole

Companion Dogs Excellent—1978

Dog	Owner
Chesaviedas Ornamental Buoy (D)	Dianna D. Blakey
Ch. Melody's Spun Smoke of Blabro (B)	Dianna D. Blakey
Ch. Z's Danny Canuk (D)	Arthur & Mary E. Mazzola
Cogley's P. R. Betsy Ross (B)	Bill Coryell
Slingshot's Bommerang (B)	B. W. & Beverly A. Hirsig

Eastern Waters Betsy Ross, C.D.X., "coming back the hard way."

Dog	Owner

Utility Dogs—1978

Dog	Owner
Ch. Chesachobee's Ovedio Millie, T.D. (B)	Dianna D. Blakey
Crosswinds Flying Orion (D)	Eunice Wynne & Walter O. Stahl, Jr.

Tracking Dogs—1978

Dog	Owner
Carolina's Cub, C.D. (D)	Charles E. Cranford
Ch. Chesachobee's Fantastic C.D. (B)	Mr. & Mrs. Ch. Cranford
Ch. Chesachobee's Bronze Atlas, C.D. (D)	R. R. McCann & M. G. Buchholz

Companion Dogs—1979

Dog	Owner
Donwen's Chesica Joy (B)	Gail Putnam
Mount Joy's Sara C (B)	Gerald R. & Roberta Sundrud
Chesachobee's Dark Sherry (B)	Mickey Tellander & Mildred G. Buchholtz
Chestnut Hill's Coke (B)	Karen W. Anderson
Cloverdale's October (D)	Joan Fisher
Lakelands Lady Terah (B)	Debra M. & Clement L. Valot
Lucy Bear's Decoy (B)	Monica F. DeBoard
Ch. Ali's Neptune Jesseka (B)	Eileen Margarette Antolino
Calbak Saba'Ka's Babe (B)	Marion G. Bieser
Ch. Kep-Ple's Atom Toko (D)	Katherine A. Kepple
Chesrite Littlrivr Nighttyme (D)	Jan M. Thomas
Chessy Kat's Beau Brown (D)	Kathleen E. Coombs
Chestnut Hills Peregrine (D)	Ronald B. Anderson
Crosswinds Flying Warhawk (D)	Jack Hoskins, Sr.
Eastern Waters Black Pt Leo (D)	Elizabeth H. Humer
Ch. Spirit of Alnwick Castle (B)	Susan L. & Michael Lamielle
Tesuque of Runkles Acres (B)	Barbara K. & Gene E. Runkle
Ch. Eastern Waters Cimarron (B)	Janet P. Horn & Elizabeth H. Humer
Z's Corky Sue (B)	Janice Ann Scandrett
Cascade Bernie (D)	Robert Gerstenfeld
Ch. Hi-Ho's Aglo Spice (B)	Ellen & John E. Schmidt & Ellen Loftsgaard
Chesavieda's Sedge Mouse (B)	Dianna D. & Jeffrey H. Blakey
Chestnut Hills Bruiser, T.D. (D)	Ronald B. Anderson
Ch. Chestnut Hills Tiger (D)	Ronald B. Anderson
Peggy of Kachemak Bay (B)	Alvin E. & Doris Davis
Teals Tule Madam (B)	Robert L. & Robin Phillips
Wulfgar of Darkenwald (D)	Rosemary C. & Kenneth M. Taylor
Z's Quail Feathers (B)	John J. & Laura McAulay
Alkarn's Duck Buster (D)	Allan R. & Karen S. Stang
Ben's Autumn Bounty (D)	Walter Pladies, Jr.
Creme De Cocoa III (B)	Robert W. Hessler
Ch. Donwens Daisy of Poisett (B)	George & Pauline E. Henshaw
Jessica Lamb (B)	Tobi Rae Carnine
Lingertot's Cocopop (B)	Shirley S. Lingertot & Carl H. Lingertot
Ch. Shugar of Cocoa Bear, C.W.D. (B)	Alberta Daugette Lowe
Thistles Flower (B)	Anne B. & Paul H. Allen
Buffy Star Gazer (B)	Freddy L. & Francine A. Sichting
Ch. Cur-san's Cinder of Marpa (B)	Sandra D. Dollar
Ch. Blustrywood's Brandywein (B)	Joan C. Littell
Cappy's Amanda of Klamath (B)	Jane Hopson
Chesacroft Cavendish (D)	Harold J. May
Heir of Alnwick Castle (D)	Michael & Susan Lamielle
Jennifer's Autumn Treasures' (B)	Walter Pladies, Jr.
Sandy Oak's Sam Hill (D)	David J. & Kathleen E. Miller
Ch. Snocre's Little Pistol (B)	Deborah A. & Charles Miller
Stormy of Shiloh (B)	Sherry Lee Massey

Companion Dogs Excellent—1979

Dog	Owner
Ch. Eastern Waters Chesaford Sun (D)	Mr. & Mrs. C. E. Cranford
Kara Allen (B)	Sherri & David A. Derr
Montauk Waters Genie (B)	Jennifer L. Cone
Chesnick's Beirdneau Lucias (B)	Janis & Jim Nicholes
Chestnut Hills Coke (B)	Karen W. Anderson
Ch. Mitsu Kuma's Rum Bun (B)	Dyane M. Baldwin & Barbara L. Mullen
Mount Joys Sara-C (B)	Gerald & Roberta Sundrud
Summer Winds Topaz (B)	Doris Hodges
Ch. Mitsu Kuma's Saxon Pond (D)	Wm. C. & Dyane M. Baldwin

Champion Count Chocula, C.D., in a pensive mood. Owner, Elizabeth Gough. Photo by M. E. Gough.

Eastern Waters Betsy Ross, C.D.X., shown here with the "Ch. Chesareid Amber Hue Memorial Trophy for Novice Obedience," which she won in 1976 by earning her C.D. with the first three legs averaging 195.6.

80

Dog	*Owner*

Utility Dogs—1979

Ch. Chesavieda's Ornamental Buoy, T.D. (D)	Dianna D. Blakey
Slingshot's Boomerang (D)	B. W. & Beverly A. Hirsig
Wendy's Miss Dusty Dawn (B)	Herbert L. Swinney

Tracking Dogs—1979

Ch. Chesafords Chestnut Newfy (B)	Mr. & Mrs. Charles E. Cranford
Ch. Oaknthistle's Albatross (D)	Dr. James V. & Brenda Stewart
Chestnut Hill's Dusty, C.D. (B)	Christine Anderson
Ch. Melody's Spun Smoke of Blabro, C.D.X. (B)	Dianna D. Blakey
Chestnut Hills Bruiser (D)	Ronald B. Anderson
Ch. Misty Morn's Cinnamon Cinder, C.D. (B)	Julia A. & Lorne M. Cole

Companion Dogs—1980

Chodam's Apache Star (B)	Mickey Tellander
Misty's Alkarn's Teal Trapper (D)	Allen R. & Karen Stang
Ch. Red Lion's J. J. Sample (D)	Mary Jane Pappler
Ch. Twin River's Riptide Teal (B)	Beverly & Michelle Millette
Crosswinds Flying Zephyr (B)	Mrs. Kimberly Ann Carey
Aleutian Sand (D)	Wm. J. & Victoria S. Fenili
Dakota City Kate (B)	Wm. H. & Norma D. Vennard
Engler's Autumn Sugar Cane (B)	Mrs. L. E. Engler & Cheri E. Storer
Wyndams Annie of Caroway (B)	Carol Anderson
Ch. Cocoa Princess Ann (B)	Robert Albaugh
Cubs Wet Water Willie (D)	Tom D. Burns
Ch. Poolside's Larena of Shiloh (B)	Susan L. & Michael Lamielle
Artemis of Paradise Island (B)	Judith M. Turner
Eastern Waters' Clover (B)	Roger L. Horn
Eastern Waters' Robin Hood (D)	Janet P. Horn & Susan K. Cone
Quellwater Inca (B)	Lori Shope
Dandee of Rimrock (B)	Joseph B. & Phoebe F. Maloney
Dogwalk's Dame Dynamite (B)	Thomas E. Adams, Jr.
Chippewa's Sunshine Playboy (D)	Robert K. & Mary T. Brown
Ch. Cub's Sonoma Mountain Jack (D)	Victor M. Reid III & Barbara T. Reid
Roseway's Rusty of Surfside (D)	David J. Illias & Nikki Berthold-Illias
Ch. Snocree Hi-Ho's Timia Lass (B)	Theresa Barton
Corky's Hershey Camelot Dame (B)	Robert P. & Linda M. Corcoran
Decoy's Miko (B)	Maurice J. Collisi
Ch. Eastern Waters Revere (D)	Mr. & Mrs. Paul W. Clark
Ch. Jonathon Livingston Seagull (D)	Nadine L. Bengel
Crosswinds Riverside Cheena (B)	Terry Behnke
Crystal The First Of Spring (B)	Alisa Godemann
All American Smokey The Bear (D)	Patricia & Walter Woodward
Ch. Duke of Dunkirk (D)	Vernica Brooks
Jerry's Flying Dixie Ruby (B)	Jerry B. Allen
Rockrun's Tule Hotrod (D)	Lewis W. Faulkner & Jerold S. Bell

Companion Dogs Excellent—1980

Jessica Lamb, C.D. (B)	Tobi Rae Carnine
Ch. Misty Morn's Cinnamon Cinder, C.D., T.D. (B)	Julia A. & Lorne M. Cole
Z's Hollow Echo, C.D. (B)	John J. & Laura S. McAulay
Ch. Chestnut Hills Tiger, C.D. (D)	Ronald B. Anderson
Ch. Sandy Oak's Sam Hill, C.D. (D)	David J. & Kathleen E. Miller
Wildwoods Son Of A Gun, C.D. (D)	Kathy Johnson & Susann Martiniuk

Tracking Dogs—1980

Slingshot's Boomerang, U.D. (B)	B. W. & Beverly A. Hirsig
Ch. Eastern Waters' Betsy Ross (B)	E. Christopher & Susan Cone

Champion Count Chocula, C.D., training for his Tracking title. Owned and handled by Elizabeth Gough. Photo by E. Towart.

Champion Calbak Black Brant Mushroom, C.D., handled by owner Rainey Weremeichik, is shown going Best of Opposite Sex at the Westbury Kennel Club Show, September 30, 1973, under judge Hayworth F. Hoch.

Left to right: Champion Chesrite Justin Tyme, C.D.; Champion Chesrite's Misty Harbor, C.D.; and Champion Seamaster's Ginger, C.D. Photo by E. Gough.

A Gal and Her Chesapeakes

While this is just a short chapter, it is also a very important one. It shows just what can be done in field, show, and obedience competition by one woman who was absolutely "green" when she received her first Chesapeake from the author and his wife. The gal is Rainey Weremeichik and she currently is one of the Eastern Regional Directors of the American Chesapeake Club.

Rainey's first Chesapeake, Judy, was six months old before Rainey had a chance to start working with her, and, as most knowledgeable Chesapeake people know, many bad habits may have been formed by that time. Fortunately, this was not true of Judy. As Rainey says, "She ruined me for any other breed."

Rainey knew little about obedience and even less about field training, but somehow she and Judy worked through together.

Although she had never attended a formal obedience training class of any kind, Judy earned her Companion Dog title in three shows, with all scores over 190 out of a possible 200.

During this time, Judy also placed in Derby Stakes in sanctioned field trials and she had twelve points toward her bench championship when she passed away very prematurely.

At this time another Chesapeake by the name of Honey Bear entered Rainey's life, and Rainey, quite naturally, wondered secretly if Honey Bear could equal Judy. But, in Rainey's words, "She gave me no time to think of that again."

Honey Bear, at ten months of age, was running in licensed field trials and placing in Derby Stakes—no less. At the same time, she was working toward her first obedience title.

Honey Bear earned her Companion Dog title in three straight shows, with scores averaging 194-2/3. She tied for first place twice. She also won the Eastern Shore Trophy for highest scoring Chesapeake.

Now came a problem that Rainey had to overcome. In working for the Companion Dog Excellent title, several of the commands clash with similar commands used at field trials. For instance, in obedience, on the retrieve for the dumbbell, the dog must come and sit in front. Then, after the handler takes the dumbbell, the dog must come around to heel position. In field training, the dog goes directly to heel position with the bird in her mouth and the bird is then taken by the

handler. This procedure gives the handler a better chance to place the dog on a line with the next retrieve.

Rainey didn't want Honey Bear to lose any points in obedience on this, so she worked out different words for the commands. This was so Honey Bear would know that one command meant for her to retrieve and then come to sit in front of Rainey, and that the other, which she already knew, meant for her to go directly to the heel position.

When Rainey threw the dumbbell, she gave the command "Fetch," and Honey Bear would deliver the dumbbell in front. When a bird or bumper was thrown, the command "Back" meant Honey Bear was to retrieve and come straight around to the heel position.

One day Rainey decided to find out whether Honey Bear really knew the difference in the two commands. First she used "Back" for the dumbbell, and the Chesapeake went right to heel before delivering. Then she threw the dumbbell again with the command "Fetch," and Honey Bear delivered it in front. She really knew the difference. This is just one instance of the fantastic intelligence of the well-trained Chesapeake.

The next problem was the "Down" command, which is taught along with a signal. In obedience, on the recall, the dog is to drop down on his way to the handler, upon command or signal from the handler. The usual signal is given with the hand straight up, then dropped to the handler's side.

To Honey Bear, this signal was a "Back" when she was being handled to a blind retrieve in a field trial. Rainey had to be very careful in devising a signal which would not confuse her dog. This is the signal she devised: with elbow bent, she places her right arm across her body, then drops it down to her side. Once Honey Bear got the idea, she had no trouble differentiating between the two commands. She finished her C.D.X. with all scores over 190 and won first place at the American Chesapeake Club Specialty Show.

Honey Bear would retrieve anything she was sent for, and in her many, many exhibitions for school children, she would retrieve a moving robot whose chest opened and sparks flew out. The children would scream with delight at seeing this.

Honey Bear had the most fun as a part of a scent/hurdling race team. In this, each dog is sent over four hurdles. At the end, all of the dumbbells of the different competitors are strewn around on the ground. Each dog has to scent out his own dumbbell and then return over the same hurdles with the dumbbell in his mouth. Honey Bear excelled at this and the team of which she was a member, retired undefeated.

Honey Bear now helps Rainey to bring along her new Chesapeakes. One of these is Mushroom, who finished her bench championship and her C.D. title at about the

Above and right: Calbak Tricrown Pony Xpress, with grace rivalling that of a ballet dancer, leaps to catch the Frisbee. Owner, Rainey Weremeichik.

same time. She earned her C.D. in three shows, just one-half point away from being the highest scoring Chesapeake in the country.

Another member of Rainey's Chesapeake family is Pony, who produced a litter from which came the newest member, Acorn.

Here is Rainey's assessment of Chesapeakes—in her own words: "I know that each one is unique in his own way. However, they all must have a feeling of belonging, and of being very much a part of you, in order to give you their devotion, as only a Chesapeake can give."

Rainey's assessment is correct. I am familiar with all Retrievers, and some of the other breeds are quite devoted to their owners, but no other dogs give one hundred percent of themselves as the Chesapeakes do.

During the course of Rainey's Chesapeake ownership, my wife and I presented her with one known as Jib. Jib was a handsome bitch whom my wife finished on the bench at the tender age of ten months. Because we were all wrapped up in field trials at the time, we felt that Rainey could give Jib more love and attention than we could, and we were right. As Rainey says, Jib was her constant companion and she actually ran her in Gun Dog Stakes, which is more than we could do. She also was an excellent guard dog, and only Rainey could open the door of her car when Jib was in it.

So there is one woman who learned about obedience, show, and field competition right along with her Chesapeakes. The Chesapeake is just the dog to do it with if you are as astute as Rainey Weremeichik.

Calbak Acorn, Winners Bitch at the 1978 American Chesapeake Club Specialty Show. Breeder-owner, Rainey Weremeichik. Handler, Peggy Long.

Above: American and Canadian Champion Eastern Waters Skipjack, C.D. and Canadian C.D., handled by Daniel Horn. Judge, Edward Squires.

Below: American and Bermudian Champion Eastern Waters Brown Charger, American and Bermudian C.D., handled by Daniel Horn.

Below: Champion Eastern Waters Baronessa, making the second of her three consecutive Best of Breed wins at the American Chesapeake Club National Specialty Shows (1964, 1965, and 1966). Breeder-owner-handler, Janet P. Horn. Judge, Louis J. Murr.

Above: Champion Chestnut Hills Pontiac winning Best of Breed at the 1977 Westminster Kennel Club Show. Owner, K. W. Anderson. Judge, E. W. Tipton, Jr.

Eastern Waters
Chesapeake Kennel

No book on Chesapeakes would be complete without the story of Janet and Dr. Daniel Horn. They founded the Eastern Waters Kennel many years ago, and they have been kind enough to send me a history of their activities—most of which have been in conformation and obedience competition. Many Eastern Waters Chesapeakes are still winning at this date.

Here then, in Janet's own words, is the history of Eastern Waters Chesapeake Kennel.

"We purchased our first Chesapeake, Gloriana II, C.D., in 1946, over thirty years ago, as a ten-week-old puppy. She developed into a truly all-around Retriever, and competed in shows, obedience, and field trials. She was more than a dog, a member of the family as most Chesapeakes are. We first used the name 'Eastern Waters' to register puppies from our first litter in 1948. Ch. Tempest of Eastern Waters, C.D., was the first of sixty champions to date to bear the Eastern Waters name, and almost as many Eastern Waters Chesapeakes have won obedience titles. We have bred and raised Chesapeakes for thirty years while living in New York, New Jersey, Georgia, Virginia, Switzerland, and Canada. About half the titles recorded here were made by owners other than ourselves. We have exported Chesapeakes to six countries in Europe and also to Canada. We have always been actively showing and training our own dogs.

"At Lancaster, Pennsylvania, in 1961, Ch. Eastern Waters Tallapoosa, C.D., handled by Dan Horn, became the first Chesapeake to win first in the Sporting Group in a show held east of the Rocky Mountains. Tallapoosa's grandson Ch. Eastern Waters Dark Knight, C.D., T.D., also handled by Dan Horn, won the Group at Raleigh, North Carolina, in 1964.

"A total of ten Chesapeakes bred by Eastern Waters have placed in Sporting Groups, including the record-making American and Bermudian Ch. Eastern Waters Brown Charger, C.D. He was owned and handled by Dan Horn and won thirty Group placements, an enviable record, especially some twenty years back.

"American and Canadian Eastern Waters Skipjack, C.D., owned and handled by Janet Horn, and Canadian Ch. Eastern Waters Little Acoma, C.D., owned and

handled by Henry J. Kudlinski, have placed in Groups in Canada, and Skipjack holds nine CACIB (*Certificat d'Aptitude au Championat Internationale*) awards in four countries in Europe.

"Eastern Waters Chesapeakes have been shown in thirteen countries in both hemispheres.

"The Horns have bred four Chesapeakes that have won Best of Breed at the American Chesapeake Club National Specialty Shows. Ch. Eastern Water's Baronessa, T.D., won for three successive years, and Baronessa's son, Ch. Eastern Water's Oak, C.D., T.D., owned and handled by Rupert J. Humer, won from the Classes in 1968 and again from the Veterans Class in 1975. Ch. Eastern Water's Brown Charger, C.D., won the Specialty in 1970, and Best of Breed in 1971 was Ch. Eastern Water's Big Gunpowder, owned and handled by William K. Boyson. The Eastern Water's Specialty record also includes three winners of Best in Sweepstakes, and five Best of Opposite Sex in Sweepstakes since 1964. Three Chesapeakes bred and owned by the Horns (Baronessa, Dark Knight, and Brown Charger) have won Best of Breed at Westminster.

"American and Cuban Ch. Eastern Waters' Nugget, U.D.T., owned and handled by Mildred G. Buchholz, and Eastern Waters' Blazing Star, U.D.T., owned and handled by Mrs. Dana Gordon, are among the first three Chesapeakes to have earned a bench title and all three of the obedience degrees. (Since Mrs. Horn wrote this, the A.K.C. has approved competition for two additional obedience titles, as explained in the chapter on Chesapeakes in obedience.) Seven additional Eastern Waters Chesapeakes have completed the C.D.X. title and eleven have earned the Tracking title. There must be over fifty that have made their C.D."

The Horns describe the Chesapeake as a great family dog, and many people constantly exclaim over how good Chesapeakes are with children. The Horns have tried to encourage this important breed characteristic by encouraging the exhibition of Chesapeakes in Junior Showmanship. Their daughter Marguerite qualified twice for competition at Madison Square Garden, showing Eastern Waters' champions in 1963 and 1967. Here are some closing words by the Horns:

"These are some of the outstanding achievements of Eastern Waters' Chesapeakes in competition. We are proud of them and grateful to their owners, who, in most cases, have become our good friends through sharing with us their pleasure in their dogs. We take equal pride and satisfaction in the many we have bred that have proven outstanding as gun dogs and family companions. Family companions our own dogs have always been, as well as afield and on the training ground, and our sons and daughters are continuing to breed, show, and hunt Eastern Waters' Chesapeakes."

Louise Belmont feeding many Chesapeakes—but is that a Poodle, and maybe a Labrador, too? Left to right: Eslar Silver Fizz, U.D.; Field Chamion and Amateur Field Champion Hi-Winds of South Bay; Amateur Field Champion and Champion Bomarc of South Bay, C.D.; Field Champion and Amateur Field Champion Con Lab Penrod; South Bay Nike; and Champion Cherokee South Bay Project, C.D.

The Chesapeake Bay Retriever in Canada

When I was starting this book, I had high hopes for an extensive chapter on Canadian Chesapeakes, but the difficulty in obtaining photographs, etc., has made it necessary to curtail this chapter a good deal.

I am indebted to Nancy Wotherspoon of Saskatchewan for most of the information included here. She has been active in Chesapeakes for about seven years and has owned Chesapeakes for more than twenty years.

The first Canadian field trial champion was Timbertown Mick (run as Cariboo Mick), who earned the title in the 1930s, but it was not until the 1950s that the breed really came into its own. This started in Edmonton when Field Trial Champion Conroy's Golden Arrow finished. He was followed by such other good Chesapeakes as Field Trial Champion Nelgard's Baron, Dual Champion Baron's Skipper Bob, Field Trial Champion Oil City Ted, and the Canadian National Retriever Champion (CNRC) of 1956, Baker's King. Baker's King, a son of Conroy's Golden Arrow, was the only Chesapeake in any country ever to win a National Championship Stake. He earned his championship in both the conformation ring and the field, thus becoming a dual champion, so his complete title is 1956 Canadian National Retriever Champion-Dual Champion Baker's King.

Among knowledgeable Canadian Chesapeake breeders there is a fairly strong bias toward American-bred Chesapeakes. With the breed having originated in the United States, the feeling prevails in Canada that most of the best dogs emanate from the States. The top living field trial Chesapeake in Canada is Nanuck of Cheslang, an American-bred import. Nanuck has earned his Canadian field and amateur field championships and his American field championship, so he is known officially as Field Champion, Amateur Field Champion, and American Field Champion Nanuck of Cheslang.

For the past few years, most of the top "show" Chesapeakes in Canada also have been American-bred dogs, campaigned in Canada for a relatively short period of time.

Early in 1977, Canada held its first Chesapeake Field Trial Specialty—that is, a field trial limited to Chesapeakes only. Most of the dogs entered were either American or from American-bred stock. The Canadian judges remarked that they had never seen such a good entry of hard-going Chesapeakes. There is a gradual movement in Canada to buy from American breeders and use American stud dogs. This, generally, has led to better running dogs, usually with better overall conformation. Naturally, there are exceptions to both of these "rules."

The first Best-in-Show award to a Chesapeake was made in Canada and, strangely enough, under an American dog show judge, the late Winnifred Heckman. Champion Queen Cocoa was actually an American Chessie but was campaigned for a short time in Canada by Jeffrey Lynn Brucker.

I asked Miss Wotherspoon about Chesapeake field kennels in Canada, and here is her response:

"At the present time there are no really top field kennels in Canada. What seems to be happening is that a field trialer owns a good dog and may keep or lease the odd brood bitch and breed a litter, but I have seen no evidence of anyone trying to develop a field trial kennel with an organized breeding program.

"Hans Kuck of Cheslang Kennels has produced three or four litters by Nanuck, and Bunny Stevens has produced several litters based on her Field Champion and Amateur Field Champion Cocoa's Tiger Cub line. But really, the overall breeding scene in Canada is not yet focused in individual kennels or lines. That may come, but at the moment the overall picture is one of hit or miss breeding with no long-term plan for line breeding and outcrossing. That is maybe why we are having so much trouble getting first-class competitors."

Following is a list of Canadian field trial champions finished to date:

1956 Canadian National Retriever Champion, Dual Champion Baker's King; Dual Champion Baron's Skipper Bob; Dual Champion, Amateur Field Trial Champion, American Field Champion Baron's Tule Tiger, C.D.; Field Trial Champion Ce-Pine Sandy Duke; Field Trial Champion Conroy's Golden Arrow; Field Trial Champion, Amateur Field Trial Champion Gypsy's Mallard of Vigloma; Field Trial Champion Midnapore's Copper Mountain Chum; Field Trial Champion, American Field Trial Champion Nelgard's Baron, C.D.; Field Trial Champion Oil City Ted; Field Trial Champion Cocoa's Tiger Cub; Field Trial Champion Prince Cocoa of Kent; Field Trial Champion Rockyview's Radar Duke; Field Trial Champion Rocky of Cal-Peake; Field Trial Champion Timbertown Mick; Field Trial Champion Toba Tiger of Peake; Field Trial Champion Chesdel Chippewa Chief; and Field Trial Champion, Amateur Field Trial Champion, and American Field Champion Nanuck of Cheslang.

Another Canadian Chesapeake also worthy of mention is Champion Pritchard's Queen of Sheba, U.D., the only living Chesapeake in Canada with the title Obedience Trial Champion (O.T.Ch.).

Eloise Heller Cherry with Dual Champion, American Field Champion, and Canadian Field Champion Baron's Tule Tiger, C.D.

Chesapeake Tales

The Chesapeake is the only breed that actually has an infectious grin that will light up a whole room, but also will scare strangers "out of their pants." Every night when I return from work I receive this beautiful big grin, and it makes the day a bit more worthwhile.

Recently we introduced a female Scottish Deerhound into our home, and, of course, to Spinner, our male Chessie. As Spinner looked at this large beast, the hair started to go up on his back. He walked toward her slowly, in the usual stiff-legged gait. Then he decided to investigate. Maneuvering around her, he sniffed and looked. His head came up and on his face was the biggest grin I have ever seen, even on a Chesapeake. They have become the best of friends and play together constantly.

I do not mean to say that every Chesapeake is so good natured. Any dog that is permitted to go untrained during the formative period of puppyhood can become a nuisance or worse. This is especially true of the Chesapeake. He needs strict early training plus a loving hand.

We have raised quite a few Chessies as well as countless other breeds in the various places that we have called home, and as I said earlier, I would sooner walk unannounced into a house where there is a Doberman on guard than one where there is a Chesapeake. The Chesapeake is truly formidable.

This brings us to our first story about the Chessie. Most are about the Chessie and hunting—for that is the best facet of this beautiful breed—but this one deals with another aspect of breed character.

Our first Chesapeake was known as Chips. His owner had passed away and the widow could not handle the dog. Chips was two years old, and had every bad habit possible, but we loved Retrievers and took Chips on.

I must explain that at the time, some twenty-five years ago, my wife and I operated a large boarding, show, and field kennel. Both of us were professional handlers in the show ring and we also ran Retrievers in field trials. This kept us quite busy.

One afternoon when I was away training, the doorbell rang. My wife answered and there stood a large fellow a bit under the weather, who forced his way into the trimming room. He was leering and obnoxious, and said he wanted to see some dogs.

Without thinking twice, my wife opened a kennel door and took Chips by the collar and walked toward the intruder. Chips grinned upon occasion, but he gave this visitor the most horrible snarl my wife had ever heard and pulled against my wife's restraining hand on his collar. The man took one look and made a beeline for the front door. He was out, in his car, and away before my wife could even start laughing.

I wish I could say that Chips turned out well, but, alas, such is not the case. He had too many bad habits. One of the worst was fighting with other dogs, and at the age of two, he couldn't be broken of it. He was a good retriever as long as he was retrieving alone, but he could do a lot of damage to other dogs.

We showed him once at Westminster and he took Winners Dog, but with his tendency to fight, even that was more a chore than a pleasure.

After Chips won a battle with an Airedale a bit too decisively, we came to the difficult conclusion that he would never be a happy dog again, now that his original owner had died. One of the hardest things we ever had to do was to put that dog to sleep.

Chips was the extreme exception that is found in every breed, but I thought it only fair to tell you about him—if only to prove that no breed is perfect.

One of the finest Chesapeakes we ever owned was Ch. Cherokees South Bay Project, C.D. "Larry," as he was known, was also the fourth leading Derby dog in the country in 1964. At that time he was owned by Louise and Augie Belmont. He was one of the best marking Retrievers I have ever seen—and I've seen my share of them.

Unfortunately for the Belmonts and fortunately for us, Larry did not take to handling very well. Louise had done all of the training up to that time and rather than send him out to a professional trainer, she gave him to us. He was one of the best presents we ever received.

For the next eleven years, through many other Chessies, Larry was our personal hunting dog and performed many feats that almost defy belief. He did require a bit of training in the transition from field trials to hunting.

One day we were cruising in our Land Rover and came across a covey of grouse. We were lucky and knocked down a few. Naturally we sent Larry in for the retrieving. He rushed out to the birds, took one sniff, and looked up with a silly grin on his face.

As a field trial dog he had been taught not to pick up anything but pigeon, duck, and pheasant. This was something new and he wasn't about to take a chance.

Well, it took us just a few hours to make him realize that whatever we shot, he was to retrieve. From then on, he did so gladly and gracefully. It was fun to watch this big Chessie moving rapidly through heavy woods, tracking a wounded grouse or pheasant. He handled upland game birds very carefully, but with ducks and geese he was much firmer, to put it mildly.

Speaking of ducks, a story comes to mind of a "fun" field trial at which my wife and I were judging. She was on the line, while I was doubling as a bird thrower out on a little island, and she used Larry as the test dog.

The series was comparatively simple. I threw a duck out to the right while my popper popped. Then I ran over to the left and threw one out there. Then I sprinted to the

Champion Cherokee South Bay Project, C.D. (Larry.)

front of the island and threw the third bird. My wife sent Larry, and then the fun started. Larry was fairly careful in clear water, but this water was muddy and he didn't want to lose his birds. I could see him clearly as he closed on the first bird. Crunch, and he swung around and headed toward shore. Twice more the performance was repeated, and the triple had been completed with no trouble. There was not a mark on any of the ducks, and my wife had no trouble with the delivery. There was one thing, however. I had thrown three live ducks into the water, and Larry brought in three dead ones.

This, of course, is a "no-no" for field trials, but I actually prefer it for hunting. Fewer birds are lost.

Where Larry really excelled, though, was in retrieving that king of the waterfowl, the Canada goose. In connection with this, two stories come to mind, both of which are almost too incredible to be believed. Nevertheless, both are true.

The first took place some years back in a large lake in the North Woods of New York State. The place would have been inaccessible without our four-wheel-drive Land Rover. There were three of us hunting, but Larry was the sole Retriever.

Leaving the Land Rover several hundred yards from the lake, we crept up to see if anything was on the water, and, sure enough, out in the middle were six Canada geese with one acting as lookout. We could see no way in the world to get a shot. What to do, what to do!

I sent my two companions to the other side of the lake and Larry went with them. Then I crept forward. When I was almost at the water's edge, the lookout goose spotted me and started to honk his warning. All six geese then started to swim away before taking flight. Unfortunately, my partners arose too quickly and the geese took to the air—fast. My wife, one of the hunters, snapped off two quick shots. One goose plummeted to the water and started swimming toward my shore as fast as he could. Larry was, to use an apt cliché, poetry in motion. He caught up with the goose with little effort and swung around. The goose started pecking and flapping. One

Guns accurately position the bird at the National Field Trial Stake. The third man is the bird thrower.

93

quick grab at the neck by Larry and there was no more fight. Larry carried that big bird the way most dogs would a pigeon. That's not the end of the story, though. As my wife and her partner walked around the lake to meet me, Larry suddenly took off and disappeared into a marshy place in the lake. This was very unlike him and we couldn't understand it. Calling was fruitless, so we settled down to wait.

About a half hour later, before really mounting a search, I glanced down the road, and there came Larry, jogging merrily along with another big Canada goose locked in his jaws.

Reconstructing the action, my wife thought she must have wing-tipped the other goose with her second shot, but only Larry saw him glide down, perhaps five hundred yards away. If our big Chesapeake hadn't been so alert and marked so well, one goose would have been lost instead of being enjoyed on our dinner table. There, my friends, is marking that you don't see at field trials.

Another story that I recall shows the tenacity of the Chesapeake over most other breeds of Retriever. This concerns a young bitch that we had as a house dog. For field trials she was impossible.

If I was training her and tried to correct her, she would run and hide behind my wife, who was throwing birds. If my wife was handling, the dog would use me for protection. If we both became angry at the same time, the dog would sit equidistant from the two of us and grin that silly grin. No, Jib was no field trial dog, but she was persistent.

One blustery November day, we were hunting off an estate on Long Island Sound in lower New York State. We had Jib along, for we had been doing some training before the ducks started to fly.

As we crouched down in the tall reeds, a pair of mallards flew low enough for me to shoot. I wing-tipped one, and it plummeted into the sound several hundred yards out. Since Jib was the only dog with us, I gave her the "Back" signal but without much hope. Was I surprised! She plunged into the choppy water and swam toward the duck, which now was so far out that we couldn't see it.

Before long, Jibby herself was just a speck on the distant horizon. We started to worry, then settled down, lit cigarettes, and waited. Even with the field glasses, both duck and dog were out of sight.

About ten cigarettes later, we really started to worry. The surf was getting rougher and rougher as the wind increased, and even though we knew that Jib was a strong swimmer, every dog, even a Chesapeake, has a limit.

Finally, after peering through the field glasses for what seemed like an eternity, I spotted something coming toward us. Soon it became a definite shape. It was Jibby and, glory be, she had a duck in her mouth. I don't know how she did it, since I wasn't out there with her, but that must have been one of the longest retrieves that any of our Chesapeakes have ever made.

Two things about that episode stay in my mind and I remember them clearly. First, Jibby wasn't even panting after she had delivered the bird, even though that was the most exercise she had all year. Second, as I roughed up her thick Chesapeake coat, I noted that although she had been in the water for at least forty minutes, her undercoat was barely damp.

That was our Jibby! If I had dropped that duck twenty-five yards out, she probably would have told me to go get it myself—but this was a challenge. Jib never got to the field trials, but my wife finished her on the bench quite easily. In fact, she placed over some of the top Eastern show dogs before she was a year old.

Jib didn't like the field training, but the shows were fun!

Since Larry was our personal hunting dog for more than ten years, I naturally have more stories about him than about any of our other Chessies. Here is another experience that comes to mind. If the game warden had caught me, I'd never have been able to convince him of the truth, and I'd just about be getting out of the "pokey" now.

This time I was alone with Larry. It was mid-December and all of the terrain was frozen except for a stream of water running fast with ice floes between the spit of land on which we were hunting and a small island some fifty yards out. It was snowing, also, as we both lay on the icy ground thinking of a nice hot toddy. At least I was thinking of one. Suddenly I heard a low moan from Larry, and I turned to see him gazing off into the distance. Looking in the same direction, I saw two swans, together with two Canada geese, swooping low over the island. It was the first time I had ever seen this combination of birds flying together. I held my shot for fear of hitting one of the swans.

When the birds made their second swoop over the island, several shots sounded off to my left, and one of the swans dropped, badly wounded. A few moments later, the "hunter" appeared and asked me if he could use my dog to retrieve his goose. Upon learning that he had just shot a mute swan, he took off before I could get his license number, and there we were—Larry and I. Larry was whining by this time, so I sent him across, while I spent the most suspenseful fifteen minutes of my life awaiting his return. He started swimming, but the ice floes were so thick that he finally had to get up on one and then leap from floe, to floe, slipping into the icy water more than once. Finally he reached the swan and picked it up rather gingerly. The trip back was even more difficult. With the huge bird in his mouth, he was forced to swim through the ice floes that buffeted him constantly. He finally came in, literally dragging the bird—and understandably, for it weighed twenty-seven pounds.

This should have been the heaviest object ever retrieved by any dog, but Larry later retrieved one that topped it. Let me tell you about it.

One nice day when the duck season had just opened, my wife and I took Larry and our aluminum boat, and rowed out to an outcropping of rock just about in the middle of a large tidal inlet. We settled down and waited. Because we had arrived well before sunup, we both dozed a bit only to awaken with a start. I had tied the rope on our boat to a point of the rock and the tide had come in sufficiently to lift the rope and release the boat. It was floating leisurely some ten feet away. What to do, what to do!

Fortunately, we had a boat bumper tied to the end of the rope and it was floating on the tide. I sent Larry out about six times, imploring him to fetch it, but he just didn't understand. By this time the boat was twenty feet away and drifting steadily toward the mouth of the inlet.

I kept screaming "bumper, bumper" at Larry, and my wife almost doubled up with laughter. It certainly looked as if one of us was in for a cold dip. Finally Larry understood. He swam out and took the bumper in his mouth and started the long pull back. The way I cheered, you'd have thought he was retrieving the gold at Fort Knox. It was a long, hard tow, for, remember, he was swimming against the drift of the boat. Finally he handed me the bumper and got out of the water, no doubt wondering what I was so excited about.

We never actually weighed the boat, but I'm sure it weighed more than the swan. Larry was a really strong Chesapeake. Imagine the strength he needed in his neck to swim and tow that boat.

Another Chesapeake with which I had much fun, even though I did not own her, was South Bay Nike. That bitch had the most diabolical sense of humor of any dog I have ever known.

We once had an old American Saddle Bred horse that we were trying to sell. He would carry a rider perfectly until a prospective purchaser would mount him. Then it was trot, trot, trot over to the nearest mud puddle and sit down. When the prospective purchaser was thoroughly immersed, the horse would look around as if to say, "What are you doing down there?" This is exactly the type of mind Nike had, both at field trials and at dog shows. I think she actually despised both.

I remember once when her owner, Louise Belmont, had Nike at a field trial. Louise had stopped on her way to the line to say hello to a friend. Then, without looking down, she told Nike to heel and walked up to the line. Imagine her surprise when she looked down, and—no dog. Nike was sitting like a little angel, or devil, back where Louise had stopped to talk.

My wife was showing Nike in the ring, but it fell to my lot to handle her sometimes. One time, on a particularly wet day, we were clumping up and down the ring in front of a judge. The ring was roped off. Nike obeyed perfectly until the last time. Once more the judge, with eagle eye, told me to move to the end and then move back. We never made it. When Nike reached the end, she just jumped over the rope and tried to keep going. I was not so fortunate. I ended up in a heap, tangled in the rope, with Nike giving me a big grin and licking my face.

Nike compiled a rather enviable record both as a Derby bitch and as a show dog, but both careers were ended too soon when surgery became necessary.

There is a hotel out on the south shore of Long Island where my wife and I always stayed when attending field trials. The owner at that time was a long-time friend from England, and he loved our Retrievers. In fact, he insisted that we keep all of them in our room, which was difficult, since most of them preferred their crates.

At this particular trial, we were running two Labradors and had two of our Chesapeakes along for company. I was exercising the Chessies about six o'clock in the morning, when out of a dense thicket a big cock pheasant went up. The Chessies became wildly excited and soon put up another. Naturally, during all of this time, my gun was resting securely in the gun rack in our car. (We always take a gun with us to the trials in the event that a situation such as this arises.)

After we went on to the trial, I couldn't get those pheasants out of my mind, so I wasn't too disturbed when my big Lab broke on the first series of the Open All-Age Stake, though that was fast becoming a habit.

When we arrived back at the hotel, I looked up the owner and asked him if we could hunt behind the hotel if we promised not to break any of his nice picture windows. He agreed readily and even promised to cook the pheasant for us if we got one.

I took the two Chessies and the fun began. They really didn't know how to quarter, but they were intelligent and remembered the birds from early morning. The cover was some of the roughest I have ever encountered, but it didn't daunt the Chesapeakes. The bitch plowed into a particularly painful looking thicket, and out flashed a squawking pheasant. It was easy to shoot. In all, we brought in three large birds and four of us feasted on them that evening—another tribute to the versatility of the Chesapeake.

The foregoing Chesapeake tales point up some of the astounding feats that this most versatile of breeds has performed. Also the fun an owner can have with Chessies.

Chesapeakes undoubtedly are the waterfowl dog supreme, and some of the hardest tests take place in upper New York State, where the winters rival those of the Midwest.

No matter what your area, though, if there are birds to hunt, and you want warm companionship to go with the hunting, the Chesapeake can't be beat!

These Denlinger books available in local stores, or write the publisher.

YOUR DOG BOOK SERIES

Illustrated with photographs and line drawings, including chapters on selecting a puppy, famous kennels and dogs, breed history and development, personality and character, training, feeding, grooming, kenneling, breeding, whelping, etc. 5½ x 8½.

YOUR AFGHAN HOUND
YOUR AIREDALE TERRIER
YOUR ALASKAN MALAMUTE
YOUR BASENJI
YOUR BEAGLE
YOUR BORZOI
YOUR BOXER
YOUR BULLDOG
YOUR BULL TERRIER
YOUR CAIRN TERRIER
YOUR CHIHUAHUA
YOUR DACHSHUND
YOUR ENGLISH SPRINGER SPANIEL
YOUR GERMAN SHEPHERD
YOUR GERMAN SHORTHAIRED POINTER
YOUR GREAT DANE
YOUR LHASA APSO

YOUR MALTESE
YOUR MINIATURE PINSCHER
YOUR MINIATURE SCHNAUZER
YOUR NORWEGIAN ELKHOUND
YOUR OLD ENGLISH SHEEPDOG
YOUR PEKINGESE
YOUR POMERANIAN
YOUR POODLE
YOUR PUG
YOUR SAMOYED
YOUR SHIH TZU
YOUR SILKY TERRIER
YOUR ST. BERNARD
YOUR VIZSLA
YOUR WELSH CORGI
YOUR YORKSHIRE TERRIER

OTHER DOG BOOKS

A GUIDE TO JUNIOR SHOWMANSHIP
  COMPETITION & SPORTSMANSHIP
THE BELGIAN TERVUREN
THE BLOODHOUND
THE BOSTON TERRIER
BOUVIER DES FLANDRES
BREEDING BETTER COCKER SPANIELS
THE CHESAPEAKE BAY RETRIEVER
CHINESE NAMES FOR ORIENTAL DOGS
THE CHINESE SHAR-PEI
DOGS IN PHILOSOPHY
DOGS IN SHAKESPEARE
THE DYNAMICS OF CANINE GAIT
GAELIC NAMES FOR CELTIC DOGS
GERMAN NAMES FOR GERMAN DOGS
GREAT DANES IN CANADA

GROOMING AND SHOWING TOY DOGS
THE IRISH TERRIER
THE ITALIAN GREYHOUND
THE KERRY BLUE TERRIER
THE LABRADOR RETRIEVER
MEISEN BREEDING MANUAL
MEISEN POODLE MANUAL
MR. LUCKY'S TRICK DOG TRAINING
RAPPID OBEDIENCE & WATCHDOG TRAINING
DOG TRAINING IS KID STUFF
DOG TRAINING IS KID STUFF COLORING BOOK
HOW TO TRAIN DOGS FOR POLICE WORK
SKITCH (The Message of the Roses)
THE STANDARD BOOK OF DOG BREEDING
THE STANDARD BOOK OF DOG GROOMING
YOU AND YOUR IRISH WOLFHOUND

To order any of these books, write to Denlinger's Publishers, P.O. Box 76, Fairfax, VA 22030

For information call (703) 631-1500.   VISA and Master Charge orders accepted.

New titles are constantly in production, so please call us to inquire about breed books not listed here.

OUT IN FRONT

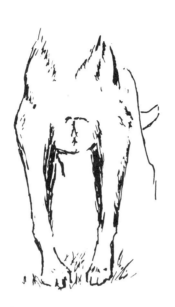

TOES IN
ELBOWS OUT

UNDERSHOT

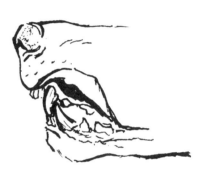

OVERSHOT

OPEN HOCKS

CORRECT HOCKS
CORRECT REAR

COW HOCKS